Strange Terrain

OTHER BOOKS BY ALICE B. FOGEL

ELEMENTAL

I LOVE THIS DARK WORLD

BE THAT EMPTY

Strange Terrain

A Poetry Handbook
for the Reluctant Reader

Alice B. Fogel

HOBBLEBUSH BOOKS
Brookline, New Hampshire

Composed in Arno Pro with Cronos Pro Display at Hobblebush Books, Brookline, New Hampshire

Cover art by Alice B. Fogel

Printed in the United States of America

Publisher's Cataloging-In-Publication Data
(Prepared by The Donohue Group, Inc.)

Fogel, Alice B.

   Strange terrain : a poetry handbook for the reluctant reader / Alice B. Fogel.

    p. ; cm.

   ISBN: 978-0-9801672-5-2

1. Poetics—Handbooks, manuals, etc. 2. Poetry—Explication—Handbooks, manuals, etc. 3. Poetry—Authorship. I. Title.

PN1042 .F64 2009
808.1   2009923107

Published by:

HOBBLEBUSH BOOKS

17-A Old Milford Road
Brookline, New Hampshire 03033

www.hobblebush.com

Contents

Step 1
SHAPE
Poems Look Different on the Page   29

Step 2
WORDS
Poems Are Made Up of Words   43

Step 3
SOUND
Poems Make Sounds out of Their Words,
Separate from What the Words "Say"   61

Step 4
IMAGES
Poems Can Make You See Things That Aren't There   77

Step 5
EMOTION
Poems Can Make You Feel Things   99

Step 6
THOUGHTS
Poems Can Make You Think   121

List of Poems

Foreword

THIS "HANDBOOK" IS unlike any book on poetry I've
read. I'm not sure it ever uses the word "interpretation,"
and I know it is not intended, as so many books about
poetry are, to train student readers to arrive at the "right"
(read: the teacher's) interpretation. There is no scansion,
no talk of metrics, no listing of latinate names for clever
sleights of hand or rare rhythmic schemes, names that a
reader may remember for the exam and then forget.

No, this is truly a guidebook to help the intelligent, amateur
reader feel more comfortable in the world of poetry. But it does
not claim to explain and erase all the mystery from poetry;
in fact, its last "Step" is intended to make the reader more at
home with that mystery, with not being able to paraphrase
or summarize it all, with "sitting with your poem."

Even readers who up till now have found poetry to be
alien, complex, and high-falutin, will be likely to get to
this last step because they have here a superb guide. Alice

By the end of
the book, this
gentle, persuasive,
sometimes
motherly guide's
aura will have
replaced the
strict, judgmental,
somber feel that
school poetry
has left in many
readers.

Fogel knows who her audience is, knows how resistant and afraid her readers may be of poetry. She is careful not to insist on certain readings or talk down to readers; instead, she creates an intimate bond with readers and frequently reminds us of the sense of fun and delight that she brings to the reading and writing of poetry. By the end of the book, this gentle, persuasive, sometimes motherly guide's aura will have replaced the strict, judgmental, somber feel that school poetry has left in many readers. Readers may not notice it, but Fogel's elegant prose includes many poetic devices, so readers will get practice dealing with metaphors and images even if they skip the poems themselves.

But don't, because one of the unique strengths of the book is that Fogel is not just a good reader and an empathic teacher. She is also a terrific poet, and she uses her poems to explain the steps and build the reader's confidence. Because she stands at the unusual vantage point of both reader and writer, she can talk with confidence about the intention, evolution, and surprise in a poem, and readers can make their own judgments about whether the poems have succeeded according to Fogel's plan or have developed a life of their own. As poet, she gets behind the words of poems to explore and make sense of meaning and feeling that "comes from somewhere beyond words." But this isn't a book of personal revelations and confessions. As Fogel says, "my preferred 'I' is more an 'eye' through which I look outward at the world." She works to give readers "faith in the justice" of a poet's choices, "so that even if you don't spend a lot of time thinking about what that reason might be, you will at least trust the poet, and therefore the poem."

If Fogel were a less accomplished poet, the book might feel like amateur recital night, with readers grimacing at the crude attempts at art. But with scores of her own poems in publication, including her national poetry bestseller *Be That Empty*, Fogel knows what she's doing, and every poem is well worth reading on its own, regardless of whether the reader learns from it the lesson Fogel sees in it. By not trotting out the classic poems of famous poets, Fogel avoids making readers feel that they should genuflect in front of monuments of culture, and bypasses the inevitable "My last teacher told me this poem was about . . ." response.

Perhaps because Fogel steers clear of classic poems and tired approaches to them, she comes to the reading of poetry with wonderfully fresh insights. For instance, she has a terrific little section on silence in poems. Spaces and stanza breaks are, she writes, "the negative space that lets us see the faces in the urns," an image I won't soon forget. And in reference to the use of familiar phrases that poets can sometimes "get away with," she writes, "Reference to familiar cultural catch-phrases lends a poem the weight of accepted thought reconsidered."

Readers who have followed the steps of this guide carefully will not reach Step 8 feeling cheated because they *still* don't have a formula for unlocking every poetry secret. Rather, armed with knowledge of how a poem's

Perhaps because Fogel steers clear of classic poems and tired approaches to them, she comes to the reading of poetry with wonderfully fresh insights.

 xi

shape, words, sound, images, emotions, thoughts, and literary devices work to build, communicate, and deepen the mystery, readers are likely to sigh with relief that there still is plenty in poetry to wonder about, to feel but not articulate, to sense but not say.

BROCK DETHIER
Director, Utah State University Writing Program

Strange Terrain

endless ideas to think about, confusions of emotions to explore, images of beauty and horror and everything in between to contemplate and share. It will surprise, delight and inform about all the ways language can be artfully arranged to viscerally express the impact of the world upon us. It will connect you to nature and civilization, other people near and far, now or then, and to your own inner life.

But it will not give you answers.

The mysterious nature of what poetry says—what often cannot be paraphrased—is its lifeblood. That doesn't mean poetry must elude us; it means the meaning of life itself often eludes us. If you want to grapple with the value of this better, you can turn to Step 8: "Unknowing," right now; go ahead—it explains in detail why poetry can't be entirely explained. The only reason it comes last in the instruction process is because it is simultaneously the least definable and most defining of the Steps.

Keeping the need for "remystification" in mind throughout may help you as you proceed on this exciting journey towards a deepening relationship between you and poetry.

* * *

Whether you are a student or a teacher or simply a traveler through life, *Strange Terrain* is a painless way for you to start over and enter the land of poetry now. It is an

The mysterious nature of what poetry says—what often cannot be paraphrased— is its lifeblood. That doesn't mean poetry must elude us; it means the meaning of life itself often eludes us.

invitation to connection and experience, and you can make use of it in a number of ways, which I'll go into in more detail in the optional "Suggestions for Discussions and Syllabi" chapter at the end. Briefly, then, here are some possibilities.

On your own or in a reading group or class, use the Step headings alone as quick guidelines for approach- · ing poetry from the inside, or else delve all the way into those Steps for more profound immersion. If you are already a reader or writer of poems, use the book to deepen your readings or your work. Teachers can use the book first (or finally) as a re-visioning tool for their own relationships with poetry, and then as a course syllabus at virtually any level, modifying for children who are very young or for time constraints, and encouraging questioning, and penciling in the margins. And critics or reviewers can use the book's topics as points of approach toward any work being discussed.

Throughout, I have included previously published poems from my first two collections, published by Zoland Books, to provide practice and illustrate specific aspects of prosody in the most literarily intimate way possible. I purposely avoid "interpreting" or telling you what I see or feel in other poets' work because I want you to experience poems on your own terms. You will no longer be a passive self-doubter but an empowered (to use the self-help vernacular) reader. When I use an individual poem here as an example of a particular aspect of poetry, I could just as well have used others, and I could—and occasionally do—include the same poem as an example of another aspect. To extend your learning, when you're ready, you can do this yourself. At that point, you will also find that almost any poem by any writer you encounter can be plugged into the Steps.

"How much time will I need to invest in order to gain from this program?" That is totally up to you and how far you want to take it.

Reading groups can share the book for discussion of either the poems or the lessons, or both, and as a basis for gatherings involving other poetry, in either a single meeting or multiple ones.

Discussion groups can cover the entire 8-step program in two hours, as I have often done. In this case, we only read and discuss a few poems, as illustrations of several of the Steps, while other Steps are simply talked about briefly. (Never skip Step 8.) I call this approach "Show and Tell," because I only "tell" about some of the Steps while others get poems to "show" their points. Still, it's enough to open most participants to a whole new relief-breathing interest in poetry.

On the other hand, an entire semester's course can easily be built around the book, with further possible options including asking students to bring in other poems for discussion of specific elements they want to explore, readings by visiting poets, and class writing assignments not only on poetry but on the reading process itself.

A good way for groups or classes to do it, falling reasonably between a single evening and a semester, is to allow four to eight meetings altogether over a period of time, dividing the Steps accordingly.

... almost any poem by any writer you encounter can be plugged into the Steps.

🌸 9

If it's just you, you may simply want to read the book straight through in your own time, taking breaks as necessary from the careful, attentive focus poetry requires. Or if you're like most people (i.e. busy), you might dip into the sections randomly and sporadically, or whenever the spirit moves you, to stimulate new thinking on any part of the book's ideas. Keep it in the kitchen for when you're waiting for water to boil—or in your pocket when you step out into the world.

Note: In each section, poems mentioned but not discussed in detail appear at the end of that section, unless otherwise stated.

Introduction
to a Poet
(& the Writing Process)

WITH A FEW words about myself, I may be able to open a window onto what poets are up to when they come to the writing of poems. People each have their own compelling ways to put life into perspective; it may be through their interest in painting, sports, kayaking, or photography. You will see that the work of poets, just like the work of so many others, blazes one kind of path through life. Just as you can enjoy a baseball game from the bleachers or from your couch, this is another path you can choose to walk simply as an occasional observer.

When I look back on my childhood, I find myself thinking that I never developed my personal love for poetry; rather it seems to me as though I was born with it. By confessing this outright, I hope to clear the table. Now you know who you're dealing with, and can get a taste for what it is about poetry that has had a different effect on me than it may have had for you. If you'll let me, I may be able to use this difference to guide those of you who grew up without poetry, or who were bludgeoned mercilessly by it.

I experienced insecurity of my own regarding poetry. People don't generally respond positively to confessions of poetry-loving. Eventually I wised up to this and went into the closet with poetry, avoiding in shame even answering the question of what I "did" or liked to do. But before that, often, like an idiot, with desperate need for even a simple nod of understanding of all that went into those words from inside me, I would hand my latest all-night, heart-felt, soul-baring offering to a friend, only to have it disappear into a black hole and never be heard of again. Once when I was sixteen, complying with my English class assignment, I shakily read aloud an entire poem I'd written about losing an old friend (relatively speaking, for being all of sixteen), the last part of which I am presenting to you here, if you can believe it; I never learn:

> I feel how an old man must
> when he throws seeds and bread crumbs
> on the cobblestone floor of the park
> for the pigeons from the peeling green bench
> all day in the sun;
> when he stands up to leave,
> they scatter and fly
> as if he were just any child
> ignorant of their ways.

And yet he comes again tomorrow,
and so do I. . . .
But you, tired and busy, and older now,
you lose a day in the sun
before even a pigeon could fly from you
or a feather blow across the grass
where we once passed—
we—you and I—who once were friends.

In the second after I uttered the poem's last syllable,
the bell rang and everyone bolted. I have rarely felt more
vulnerable than I did at that moment in the blur of my
classmates' fleeing bodies.

For all I know, you were one of them.

Let's be friends now.

I was not about to give up poetry in exchange for
popularity, but neither did I retreat to literature's seduc-
tion out of loneliness. I chose poetry first, and relation-
ships would have to share me, even if it meant meeting
with poetry illicitly at the No Tell Motel.

To tell you now about my unwitting beginnings as a
poet, I have to go back to my absolute earliest, and much
happier, memories, because I loved poetry before I tech-
nically knew what it was, and began to write just as soon
as I could make the proper scratches with a pen. Why?
To make a long story short:

My first memories are of my solo weekend visits to
the small Brooklyn apartment of my paternal grand-
parents. On Friday nights my grandfather dovened,
wrapped in his black leather bonds and white shawl,

praying hypnotically in a low chant while my grand-
mother waved candlelight into her eyes. To me, three
years old and being brought up secular American in a
small suburb, the world of these Orthodox Jews was a
foreign one. But the warm, intimate intensity of the dark-
ness there, punctuated by small flames and strange mur-
mured sounds, also made it feel like home.

I understood—instinctually, of course; not verbally—
that that not-quite-melodic, not-quite-random music
was another language: not merely the Hebrew, but prayer
in Hebrew, with its own ancient lilt and sway. I think of it
now as the archetypal rhythms of a mother rocking her
child, the song—geographic, ancestral—of life on this
earth. I fell in love with it: alert lullaby, audible, rhythmic
runes, the deep meaning of purely emotional sound that
with experience might become literal as well. "Sea Gull"
(page 15) is a poem that strives for this same effect.

Sea Gull

Needle, icicle, flash of eye
        in light   this swift
  shape of white
        caught me in its wing-
span   out-spun, overhead,
                inland.
It traced a high arc
        sparking winter sky,
  sewing its sharp
        quick stitch
on raised eyes'
        air   and carved
a new design at the darker
                edge of sight
  across the slower beauty
                of an unmoving
afternoon moon.

If this poem seems like just a bunch of sounds and quick, undeveloped images, with nothing to hold onto as far as "what is going on," that's because that's exactly what it is. In other words, "what is going on" in this poem *are* its sounds and quick images—my impressions of a sea gull on that particular day.

I was lucky to have parents that both directly and indirectly supported my budding affair with language as song, and helped develop its literary counterparts, partially through their own love of reading. Over time, I found that writing was the most doable art to pursue of all those I loved: the materials were minimal and cheap, and there didn't need to be any audience until I went looking for one (and not always even then). Writing challenged me in how it encompassed so many elements of other arts—movement, form, sound, image, sense and sensation, even thought and emotion.

Why poetry and not prose, then? That intensity, again; language as tool to manipulate both mind and heart, though not necessarily in the service of any narrative. The snapshot of the human condition, of our mortality reflected in nature; the staying of time.

Or: Why poetry and not prose? I don't know. Why baseball and not soccer? Why brain surgery and not radiology? Why real estate and not shoes?

Poetry has always been with me, and I expect it always will be. Its scintillating additions to my life more than make up for the empty stares of acquaintances. But you don't have to be born into poetry to enjoy reading it, or even writing it. Old dogs often do learn new tricks, and you will too, counting poetry among the available ways to gain an articulated acknowledgment of your own far-reaching thoughts and feelings about the joys and challenges of life.

I have had to learn new tricks in order to keep writing, adjusting my writing process to fit the size of the free time allotted me over the years. I am still motivated by many of the same obsessions and inspirations—music, science, philosophy, nature—as when I was younger, but with age, work and family I have had to shrink my former all-night, leisurely writing feasts into compressed mini-binges with the muse, doing some of my "pre-writing," or brainstorming, internally until I can sit down with only myself and a page. To help put your encounters with poems into some context, let me tell you now where it is that poems "come from" for me, and what I do with those visitations.

One way a poem can arise is from a familiar word or phrase, read or overheard as if for the first time, sparking an impulse to play out a new "scenario" that might redefine it, or triggering a thought or feeling I want to explore. (The poems I mention now, unless otherwise noted, appear in the final section of the book.) "Stone Walls" (page 168) happened when the man who became my husband simply said one day, "I want to build stone walls with my father." "Unlocking" (page 169) took the New England term for the season when ice and snow finally begin to break up and turned it into a metaphor for what might happen to people if they were to free themselves that way.

One way a poem can arise is from a familiar word or phrase, read or overheard as if for the first time, sparking an impulse to play out a new "scenario" that might redefine it, or triggering a thought or feeling.

🌿 17

Likewise, a new thought or bit of factual information, especially scientific, inspires me. "Instead" (in Step 4, page 94) came from learning that dragonflies have 20,000 eye units, and imagining what that might be like. "What Birds Hear" (page 171) came out of a book I read that made me think about birds in a way I never had before. The thrill is in getting outside of the familiar, of myself, and playing make believe.

Sometimes I start from only a mood, possibly stirred up by a piece of music, so that I want to write something that might possess the same emotion. To convey that mood I will have to come up with something visual or experiential, real or imagined; you can't do much without one or the other—or as the poet and doctor William Carlos Williams said, "No ideas but in things." In "Bells without a Church" (page 172) I gave a field of wildflowers to joy. Other times there's already a picture in my head, from "real life" or otherwise, like the fog over the water in "Nelson Bog" (Step 5, page 106) and these may in turn evoke a feeling I want to spend a little time with.

Writing a
poem—and,
by proxy,
reading
it—is an
opportunity
to pay
passionate
attention
to things, a
variation on
love.

Many, if not most, poets delve into their own present or past for subject matter. Early in motherhood, I found this happening to me, as in "Learning to Read" (in Step 2, page 58)—but in general it's not my own life I most want to write about. Writing a poem—and, by proxy, reading it—is an opportunity to pay passionate attention to things, a variation on love. In some of the poems in this book I do turn my attention to personal events or relationships in my life, forming them into a kind of story or a momentary impression, and (hopefully) universalizing them. But my preferred "I" is more an "eye" through which I look outward at the world. Of course, what I see is colored by that "I."

Most of my poems, then, are not particularly auto-biographical in the usual sense; what intrigues me and many other poets most in writing is the inter-relatedness of images, sounds, rhythms and associations that words can make happen. Even if I do write from experience, I may focus on the use of language to create a piece of art broader in reach than the tale told, as in "Spring" (page 173), where I compare the season to children, including the language of cloth to tie the two together. So while a reader might see that this is a poem about the wild nature of childhood (which it is), I see it just as much as a poem about the wild possibilities of words.

As a painting is just as much "about" paint—its application onto a surface and the forms it creates—as it is about its subject, so a poem is just as much "about" its word choices and structure as it is about *its* subject.

You will find that while I'm not into photorealism here, neither are my poems abstract expressionism. Naturally, there are other poets who do write poems that might be compared to these artistic styles, and you will get enough experience with poetry here to appreciate that range.

Finally, I invite you into my room, or under my tree, to witness the actual writing process, which, possibly over a series of many days, might go like this:

I sit down with a simple "resource" (an image, piece of information or fact, even just a mood, or a combination of two or three I want to connect) usually having no idea what I will make of it, just for the sake of playing with it, and, nearly in a kind of trance state you might call the "zone," I proceed—stretching, molding, shaping the stuff at hand, like clay on a wheel. Eventually I'll stand back to see what I've made. That's a draft, or maybe three.

Then I will bring a more conscious presence of mind to bear on what I'm doing, pulling, removing, rearranging, adding, taking into consideration what the poem seems to want to tell me, encouraging an inherent unity within its own emerging sense and sensations. That might be a few or many more drafts.

Eventually, I become an editor or reader—an informed one, of course—and examine the whole for cracks, bulges, beauty, symmetry, or jarring dissonance. The list of aspects I attend to will make your head, or at least your eyes, roll. They include (but are not limited to) the rhythms and effects of punctuation, spacing and shape, lines and line breaks, stanza breaks and syllable stresses; the grammar, diction and linearity of voice and thought; and all possible conscious and subconscious interpretations of words, references, ideas and perceptions. I know, I know, the task is impossible, but poets work their material hard, trying to say everything in one brief poem, trying to make a long story short.

And voilà—however imperfect, a new form emerges, a structure for content previously ungathered in just this way.

What was it like while I was immersed in that process? I was having the time of my life. Even when the content is sad or harsh, I feel rejuvenated hope, having made something of it. People talk about writing being a lonely profession. There you are, in your cold garret, just you, staring out the smudged window at a world you can't focus on, let alone enter. You sigh, look down at the few words you've managed to eke out onto the wrinkled paper before you, scrawl out a few more, sigh again, lift your head again.

Do other writers really feel so miserable? I've never asked anyone else, but as a writer, and reader, I have never felt that proverbial kind of loneliness, and in fact have warded off the blues by way of writing and reading. Words and their acrobatics are fabulous company.

Of course, there are worthy poems that make themselves clear and felt right away. Poetry comes in a vast array of styles, from plain speech and straightforward to complex or "difficult," including those that seem straightforward but are in fact complex, and why should we avoid one in favor of another if any might be capable of touching us?

With experience, you may not have to read even a more challenging poem five times before you are speaking its language. On the other hand, a poem that can be read once and grokked entirely is not usually a poem I'm particularly interested in either reading or writing. I want to know, how was this apparent simplicity achieved? Or is it merely simplistic and therefore nothing I need ever return to? I like a challenge. I like expecting that if I spend time with a poem, I will feel and see more than I did at first. The process is interactive. I like feeling and seeing.

True: Sometimes a poem never yields any salient results; it's probably a placebo. But as long as it's given me a stirring sensation that makes me know I'm alive, piqued my thoughts or feelings, even if it still feels incomplete or incompletely understandable, I'm going to give myself over to it, get involved in discovering more about it, having faith that then it will give more of itself to me. I like poems that don't ever feel finished for me, or with me— poems that retain their beauty with age, and continue to fill me with, if not mystery, then at least wonder at how much happens there.

Poetry is a complex art form, made up of many elements that can be studied endlessly in any number of excellent books on the subject. My intention here is not

My intention
here is . . . to
start you on
your own
path through
poetry.

to load you up on the epithalamions, macaronics, anaco-
luthons and dactylic heptameters (though I might throw
in a few enjambments and metaphors) but to start you
on your own path through poetry. It is my hope that,
after thinking over what I'm saying about the rewards
of taking on poetry's challenge, and acknowledging how
different that process is from that of most reading, you
will forgive yourself for your past unsuccessful encoun-
ters with it and give it another try. After all, poetry isn't
here for us to "get" it; it's here to join us on the journey
we call life.

Step 1

⚕ SHAPE ⚕

Poems Look Different on the Page

BUT YOU ALREADY knew that. See how easy this is?

When you look at a poem you can readily see that it looks different from most things we read. The left hand margin often lines up neatly, but the right one almost never does. Sometimes even the left hand margin is jagged. What's up with this?

Poems used to rhyme; they were originally actual songs, and a useful way to remember stories, events or important personages. Rhythm and rhyme make information more catchy, which is why we often have commercial jingles stuck in our heads so annoyingly. Ending lines of poetry with a word that's going to be rhymed later on, or making the line itself a single phrase, contributes to that ease in memorization. We don't use poems for these purposes so much anymore, but some of the same explanations still apply. And, just as teenagers have fun twisting the point of what you say for their own excuses, poets enjoy choosing different reasons to shape their poems. Doing so can create interesting underlying tensions or expectations in a poem, especially if you know that we're still at least subconsciously getting a kick out of breaking old-fashioned rules.

But let's stick with the traditional for a moment more: Existing formats for poems, like sonnets or sestinas, lend necessary shapes, and poets still like to force their creativity into them, even if sometimes doing so while simultaneously bending some of their rules. "Pattern" (page 31) is an example of a form called the villanelle.

You don't need to learn the rules or names of forms, but it doesn't hurt to look over the shape of a poem initially, simply to acquaint yourself with its structure, scanning for any patterns of rhyme or repetition, or looking for more open weaves or dense construction. You'll ready your concentration accordingly, just as you settle differently on a bar stool, an airplane seat, or an old couch.

In introducing "Pattern" here for its shape, I will say a few things that will also introduce you to almost all the other Steps, so hang onto your hat. And don't worry if you're unsure of your footing as I walk you through this poem; we're still reading to focus mainly on how poems look, not what they "say."

the orchids are in bloom.

                                       In my room

when the door opens

                              feathers of snow

                                                     fly

into my arms like lovers

                              and disappear.

Then you

                  step in

                            from out of the whirled,

lay down with your white bouquet,

breathe the scent of sleep.

Always Moving

O the intemperate pulse and dance
Of these seasons so in love, moment
To moment moving
Free of holds and wholly held,
Unattached and so a part
Of belonging. Summer's scent unhinged
And set to traveling, sent afar
By wind. Laughter. Listen:
Those nomad moorings, those petalled
Pourings of morning storms: Autumn,
Passionate, impatient,
Is speaking

Of space invisible, divisible, defined
By what is passed, what present.
This is the weather poring over us
In the ecstasy of its unpredictable
Piety. October. November.
What a way to awaken!
Suddenly I know, yes, how it is
That the leaves from sheer beauty
Can dash themselves to earth,
So wonderful in how it moves
Always, in how moving
Is the world.

Morning Glory

And then,
    to find a way
        outward, to believe
           in opening.
After the long
    quick climb, viney reach,
        offshoot, curtain green,
           to be
a defiant hand,
    offer translucent
        umbrellas
           unspun against the light.
After the sharp
    nipple of bud that pushes
        out hard and
           carefully wrapped,
petulant,
    and thick
        with peaking life,
           to find
the other way, to turn
    outward against the turn,
        the same way a skirt
           unwinds after the twirl:
This is already the end, the dance ended,
    only one moment more, the moment
        of applause; this last
           incidental motion, mere encore.

To open is less a believing than no
        or yes,
                is more a giving up of one will
                        to another,
the same as the spiral of pinecone
        that lifts its
                skirts to let fall
                        the seeds,
the same as the hailstone
        designed by the flick of wind's wrist
                unwinding
                        through insistent air.
Leaf curl, fern furl, curve of lock or twist
        of fate.
                So much planning
                        and intent,
so much spent, such a
        time becoming,
                so much of and beautiful this
                        briefest blue.

The Archer

The swaying moon
frees itself scythe-like
from the forest.

When I look to you, the ring
of other nights encircles me
as if from memory

or by heart.
Like the moon, you
step into darkness
                    whole.

I see you lift your bow, hear
delicate feathered arrows shift
in your quiver. This
shot sings with a linear
precision.

The moon falls into me.

Step 2

⚕ WORDS ⚕

Poems Are Made Up of Words

IF YOU REMEMBER that, earlier, I practically said poetry is not made up of words, forgive me. I'm really not trying to confuse you. ("Do I contradict myself? Then I contradict myself," said Walt Whitman.) I meant what I said; I was making the point that we need to apprehend poetry at a depth beyond the surface of the page, because it comes from somewhere beyond words. Now I'm making a different point, which is twofold. Again, we'll start with the simple and obvious one: There are these very familiar things talking to us when we read a poem, the tools of the writer: words.

In "Please" (page 45), none of the words are particularly difficult to understand. The poem is a gentle

⚕ 43

... how do words
do that—shift
gears without
warning as they
head down
the road?

argument, starting with the title plea, which later turns into a verb—to please—after we realize we're not just talking about apples here. In regard to syntax *and* change of focus, how do words do that—shift gears without warning as they head down the road? Or maybe there is some sign of foreshadowing: The second line ends on the word 'perfect,' which you might associate with a nice specimen of apple, but when in the next line you're told that its perfection is in its vulnerability, that's probably not what you were expecting.

Please

Hold closely the red, round, sleek,
solid sphere of apple, perfect
in its vulnerability to earth and air.
Inside, seed and flesh
lurk in secret slumber, as if waiting.
But not waiting. Something could grow
out of this, something could burst it apart
from what it seems. Each seed
has a story to tell that it will never tell,
that it hasn't yet lived or learned.

The body is a globe, whole,
contained and fragile.
What it doesn't know is more immense.
You can't surprise it with predictions.
Right now something inside may be swelling,
reaching outward, working
on its own small life.
Maybe one dark seed
snaps open against your fear —
a sudden awakening into night.

You could die of knowing
or of not knowing, or —
smooth the skin against your palm,
slide your nail along its continuous curve,
its utter sheen, while your hand
trembles and dares to go on.
Smell its apple smell of wine

and earth and bowl, get its wet envelope
everywhere in your mouth,
such a dangerous delight.

You have to let in the small wonder
of apple, you have to let please
whatever can please you, hold it
skin to skin, dearly, so the wholeness
of its life passes through yours,
healing as it breaks its way
between the walls of cells.

Later on, after you finish the poem, you might be able to go back and see that the speaker (not me; the poem's persona) had in mind all along that to live life fully means embracing our built-in ignorance of some of its processes, since being open to all of life requires being vulnerable. But to swerve right into a Big Idea like that, without any visualizable markers to begin with, would probably cause a crash, leaving no one around to go for the ride.

When a writer plays with words, it can be a set-up, so keep alert as you read, just like in life, and at the same time let yourself be taken.

I take words so seriously to heart that I once spent a full ten minutes contemplating the mysterious phrase, "asnow strom" that a student wrote in an essay about skiing. I figured it was some advanced Swedish technique I hadn't heard of yet, or his private mystical mantra, until it dawned on me it was in fact a typo. He meant "a snow storm."

"Learning to Read" (page 58) and "Echoes" (page 48) directly address how words figure in our lives.

Echoes

Flat against far walls there is always a sadness
waiting to be felt, waiting to hear its name.
You call out to it and—good company—it answers.
You find a reason—the sadness enters it
like swallows swooping through barn doors.

Every open space lies between the boundaries
of bodies: parent, lover, mountain, room.
I have heard the sounds that rocks and hills
throw back at me.

When the tilted leaves, for instance, whirl upward
before rain, what happens behind my tongue
is like an aperture clicking open, open,
until the mouth has carved a cave for words.

Now I listen for some echo of organs piping sound
from hollow suites, repeating beneath my own skin.

Long before buildings, sidewalks or streets
the wild landscape met its occupants halfway.
The pigeon was a parrot in full color.
When the world grew gray, so did its feathers.

Now the city bird mimics the walls that house it
and only its sleek neck reflects the spectrum
still invisible in the sky. In my throat
I form a word, take it back, let it go.

In the beginning: my mother calls me in for supper.
I answer her with her own words and tone.
She sends out my name from the back kitchen stoop;
I return it from the front yard.

Between the gray pavement of Justamere Drive
and the gardened walls of my home, I learn
to fill my small life with whatever I am given,
and then pronounce its sounds.

Alice? Alice. Where are you? Where are you.
Question and reply, demand and counter plea.
Come here! Come *here*. I can match myself
to anything, one-to-one, world to word, a window
through which brightened birds take flight.

Even sadness
can feel good
once it is
named, even
dull-feathered
birds brighten.

"Echoes" is more autobiographical than most of my poems. I really lived on Justamere Drive when I was little, and really played this echo game with my mother once, thinking I was brilliantly fooling her. But the concept of echoing one's mother goes beyond the literal, doesn't it, and my budding sense of power involving word-play had an element of magical thinking; it echoes the Biblical rendition ("In the beginning...") of things coming into being by means of the Word ("world to word"). Even sadness can feel good once it is named, even dull-feathered birds brighten. In the poem, many kinds of "echoing" happen.

The meanings of words are simultaneously familiar to us all, and strangely malleable. That's the second aspect of how poems are made up of words—that words do new things here that yank us out of our usual expectations of them. This takes practice in poetry, not only for writers to control but for readers to fully take in.

In one sense you could say that writing poems in which words have variable or multiple meanings is an evasion. Why don't we just say what we mean and get it over with? But we may be trying to say things that *are* variable and multiple, as well as attempting to observe things that can't be approached head-on. Staring right in the eye of some aspects of life makes them look away, like a dog. In poetry, we are saying what we mean, but we may be doing so by saying something else we also mean.

Metaphor is one way to perform this sleight of hand. With metaphor, you can say two or more things at the same time, slipping under someone's skin via physical images, archetypes and sensations rather than knocking

Why don't
we just say
what we
mean and
get it over
with?

Did I want to write a poem about relationship challenges (which is what this poem is ultimately "about") or did I simply want to get inside what a grassfire might feel like (which is also what it's about)? In my case, it's usually the latter, the concrete element, that inspires me, and the abstract sneaks in. I find it more dramatic this way, as well as a lot more fun. I get to be a grassfire, a dragonfly. I get to connect myself to the things of this world.

In "Grassfire," you don't have to know I was at some point thinking about that difficult relationship; the feeling of it will sneak into you just as it did for me. Metaphorically, everything I say about the fire is also being said about troubles heating up in a relationship—not literally but emotionally. How it makes you feel like you can't breathe, like you're caught in an undertow. Along with descriptive terms, I also chose specific people-oriented vocabulary with "uh-oh" connotations: "blurted secret," "wounding," "weeping," "blame," "come clean." While you might not consciously pick them out as such, the result has a subliminal effect. This grassfire is a bad place to be, but a real intimate relationship is not as dangerous as it might feel; if I surrender to it, the poem suggests in the end, maybe new growth will follow.

Words are doing some other things in this poem. Sounds get repeated or compared ("here," "air," "hurled," "hurt," "hurtling," "blurted,") and play off each other ("coil" / "unravel") so that there's a whirlpooling sense of movement, which in turn mimics the subjects' feeling of being unable to disentangle. Even little parts of words can do this subliminal, emotional work, furthering the

Step 2
WORDS

I find it more dramatic this way, as well as a lot more fun. I get to be a grassfire, a dragonfly. I get to connect myself to the things of this world.

poem's effects, such as in how the many "uh" sounds in the first half's words give way to "oo" sounds and finally "ahs" ("entice it on to the pond for its denouement") so that, with the fire's quenching, relief seems to take over where fear and pain once reigned.

In addition to conveying so much through syntax, sound, vocabulary, play, and metaphor, words can serve the simple purpose of reminding us of things we already know, as in the opening line of "Archaeology" (page 55). By referring to the miracle of walking on water the poem shows how wondrous it is that so much goes on under our feet on land.

Archaeology

I live in this miracle of walking on land:
deeper than oceans, its waves of clay and sand
carry me. Layers of old leaves and time,
leavings of other deaths and lives. Leavening.
Sponge of humus, clumps of stone,
tiny wildlife—on these we float:
on loam upon loam upon loam.
Soil is our source and destination: home.
Civilization, Atlantis, insect histories:
this year, again, buried treasure helps to feed us.
Easily moved, easily lifted, by weather, shovel, hand—
so easily earth supports me. Primitive, thick,
original every day: a heritage of sweet dough
handed down the generations. This spring,
the garden plot lies down lightly underfoot,
and tolerates my work. It is good
in my fingers. It loosens my fist like relief.

Which
would you
rather hear:
"I love you"
or "I am
enamored
of you"?

Writers have to be aware as they make their choices that words come with their own references, including all the myriad meanings in their etymology, and their Latin, Greek, Anglo-Saxon or other roots. For instance, are synonyms really interchangeable? Which would you rather hear: "I love you" or "I am enamored of you"? What about homophones and other word associations? Because of contemporary cultural references, I can't convince my kids that they should eat whole wheat bread for its healthy "germ" without them thinking I'm trying to give them the flu.

There is much that we aren't consciously aware of when we read words, but they have their effect on us nevertheless, just as germs do. In general, when we are experienced readers of literature, we get more enjoyment from it because we "hear" voices in our heads that speak with varying tones depending on the words on the page. Although those little black marks on the page look the same, we can hear anger, sarcasm, tenderness, grief, or enthusiasm. This is really amazing if you think about it.

Back in the old days when television was new, shows had to announce when a commercial was coming on, as in "Now a word from our sponsor." With no prior experience watching the box, people couldn't tell the difference between the actual show and images being presented for another purpose. It was all one. No one has to be told now when it's a football game, a sitcom, a made-for-TV drama or a car commercial we're seeing, and if anyone tried to, we'd laugh.

By a similar process, perhaps bolstered by an innate

capacity to learn it, with experience we recognize not only meaning but tone when we read. And everyone knows that tone is even more important than words; if you sound mad at me, it doesn't matter that you're saying "I love you." I won't believe you.

The word is to poetry what paint is to a painter: Everything is translated through it.

Listen to the difference in tone, achieved through the manipulation of words through sound, diction, syntax and line, between "Archaeology" and "Always Moving" (in Step 1, page 38). Both are celebratory, but one has a quiet, almost conversational wonder, and the other is excited and impassioned. Also, look at the last word in "Always Moving"—"world." Because this poem is enraptured with autumn and its wind-blown leaves, that word is also "whirled." In the phrase "how moving / is the world," in which "moving" takes on more than one meaning, we hear both through association, just as we hear both "whirled" and "world" though only one is written.

Perhaps you've seen this on the back of a car: "Visualize whirled peas."

Context may be everything, but only if you know it; soon you will be as well versed with poems as you are with bumper stickers and TV.

Learning to Read

I remember when each word was a tiny drawing,
the perfect work of art: ecstatic carvings,
exotic lines, simple curves conducting
an inaudible opera on the page.

I remember suddenly knowing that my mother
didn't see the black markings, their meanders
through white valleys; she saw sounds,
even things: she saw a boy, a boat, a tree.

Now, at 3, my son's letters are still mobile,
unleashed to direction left to right,
and without pedestals — like Inuit sculptures
meant to be held, every which way, in the hand.

So a 3 is an E, W is M,
why must there be a 6 and a 9—they are one
and the same. Learning to read—
not evening meaning to—

we tie down the forms, tell them which way
to go. They lose most of their freedom
while we gain much of ours.
Loving the story, his hand caresses the paper

with the same yearning tenderness as mine
smoothing hair from his brow—
as if he could touch what the words say,
as if he could feel in his hand the world

that speaks to him so strangely
with his mother's familiar voice.
In my own old, best, repeated dream
I float down a river on an open book,

reach the greening shore in spring,
and hear the Mother Voice call my name.
It is the voice of earth and sky, sailing,
blowing through the leaves of the book.

It is the voice of the home
where I want my son to go
whenever he leaves home.
Whenever he learns another word,

every gain of his is my gain
and my loss, every celebrated step
full of mourning for its footprints
left behind. My hands, full of joy,

pause in their applause, positioned as in prayer:
Please, don't grow up too fast. Words,
those broken twigs, those forked rivers,
those unpaved roads, will carry him

away from me, to other lives.
There is not enough time to hold him
without holding him back—the way I could
in that brief time

when meaning had no name.
Even these words, carved so deep and hard
by the circular motion of my hands,
can never spell out enough love.

Step 3

☘ SOUND ☘

Poems Make Sounds out of Their Words, Separate from What the Words "Say"

IF YOU'VE BEEN reading right along, you've probably realized by now that there's no point trying to completely detach any aspect of poetry from any of the others. The **words** that get **shaped** into poetry by means of certain writerly **devices**, in order to entice readers to **think** or **feel** or see **images**, immerse us in the **sounds** we hear in the poem, which in turn connect with our emotions, sometimes throwing us into the realm of the **unknown**, and so on. So it's natural that we've already covered some aspects of poetry's sound in previous sections, beginning with my memories of my grandfather's hypnotic prayers.

☘ 61

Poet Donald Hall has said when we read a poem silently to ourselves we should move our lips, feeling the words in the throat. Doing so makes us imbibe more fully the juiciness of the words: They enter our bodies, not just our minds. You know that we move our tongues, our faces, sometimes our whole bodies, differently for every segment of a word. Check out Darwin's hilarious photographs illustrating the faces and gestures of nineteenth century blokes (and blokettes) uttering various sounds. His research on humans and other mammals provides evidence that words frequently evolved from sounds that we made (make!) naturally to demonstrate a feeling. When we say "snarl," for instance, we curl our lips to bare our teeth exactly as a dog does when he snarls.

Meaning, feeling and sound are mutually inextricable. Poems remind us that language is physical, not just mental.

Perhaps the most obvious—and therefore least acknowledged—sound effect in poetry is the one that comes from the shape, the broken lines terraced with spaces and stanza breaks: silence. In varying durations, silence can reflect flashes of awe, confusion and speechlessness in the face of experience, the disconnect in our efforts toward relationship or understanding, moments of contemplation, recognition, or doubt. Entirely necessary pieces of a controlled pattern of rhythm, pacing, tone and mood, pauses shape time (timing) and become complex parts of speech comparable to rests in a musical score. They also, through the power of omission, shape sense. Try to imagine music without them. Or comedy.

Pauses are the negative space that lets us see the faces in the urns.

A pause followed by an unexpected word or phrase wakes us up, like the timing and delivery of a punchline. A sentence that stops mid-attempt, particularly if never finished, by breaking the promise of expected satisfaction makes us hear the loss, the void. In a poem, read these spaces; don't skim over them as if they weren't there. If poets wanted you to read the things as prose, they would have written them that way.

Along with spaces and their silences, other aspects of rhythm like accented syllables, syntax and phrasing, rhyme, repetition, long vs. short words, consonants vs. vowels, even long vs. short vowels, all carry the sensate beat of meaning. In paying attention to sound, we go beyond the word, the way a scientist goes beyond the molecule or even atoms to look at the most miniscule iotae. So turn your microscope, and microphone, to the littlest subpoetic particles now, and to the melodies of speech they compose.

You will often see on poetry collections' book jackets that some blurber refers to the author's "music." In each case, you might have to listen for the particular musicality of that writer's style. Many are so subtle I confess I don't hear any more there than I do in common speech, though that can demonstrate some nice sounds too, sometimes delightfully surprising, sometimes plain and comforting, and almost always fraught with meaning. Everyday speech could very well be transcribed onto a

In paying attention to sound, we go beyond the word, the way a scientist goes beyond the molecule or even atoms to look at the most miniscule iotae.

musical staff. Some voice songs are multicultural—as in the falling two-syllable call of a mother wanting her child to come home, her rising two-tiered call when she's getting exasperated, or the teasing "naa naa" of one kid to another.

How a writer uses words and pauses and their aural elements is her *voice*. But you might want to know, when I write a poem, do I always make choices involving sounds and pacing consciously, or does it just come out that way? Since—sorry—the answer isn't straightforward, let's look at a few poems to see how the process works.

But first, a note about reading aloud is in order. It's important to remember to read poems in a different way from how we read newspapers or even novels. To truly appreciate not only sound but the meaning and emotion it carries in a poem, we need to break our speed- or prose-reading habits, and the best way to do this is to read out loud. Reading a poem is reading not for the destination but for the journey. Try it with the poems in this chapter—or any others at hand. Remember to "read" the spaces, too, by pausing in them.

"Which Way the Winds Blow" (page 65) came from two images that overlapped in me. One is a famous, quietly horrifying photograph from perhaps the forties that shows a man and woman on a stretch of otherwise abandoned beach, accompanied by a caption telling us that their child has been swept out to sea, which of course totally changes how you see that picture. The second is a simpler elemental intrusion, snow blown into an open, deserted home.

Which Way the Winds Blow

What hand opened the door, I don't know. No one
lives there in winter and I was only passing by. And I don't know
if it was for entrance or for exit that the place opened, or was opened.
The lake lay frozen, the sky
still as folded wings. And everywhere snow

blown into the rooms, strewn across the braided rugs
and knotty boards, under chairs, creeping
like a slow cold tide, white and silent, out of its element

with greed. At the threshold, gripping the latch, I was caught
by the photograph inside, black and white on the peeling wall. What eye
first watched that scene, taking it in, shameless, I don't know,
but I do know that boundaries were broken:

A woman, her grey dress blowing toward land,
lost on the shore in the dim light of her long day's end,
and a man, farther up the beach, alone. The sea—
mute, infinite entity—taking in its borders hungrily

and the stolen child—so said the caption—it drank up when each
entered the other in a moment
of dropped vigilance. In this kind of world no blueprint

instructs us how to house what we love
against the winds of loss. The woman, the man,
their child gone—slipped from the home of their love,
swallowed whole. I am not going to try to feel

what that woman felt, or to speak with her voice. I don't know
what she did next or how she did what she did next.
She is the mother, my fear, all the love ever lost to grief.
Her pain is an ocean vaster than planets, a diaspora

of longing flung to all four flogging winds. In her life,
I am sure that time drifted past her, with her, within her.
I know that that summer, like all summers, moved on
through the fall into winter, that the shore closed up,
abandoned, cold. And that the thing lost

still blows through us, the swollen door no longer shuts.

When, as a mother, I tried to put myself in the place of the woman in the photograph, I wrote, "I don't know / what she did next or how she did what she did next." It's an unusually long string of single syllable words that, reading it, slows us down to feel the weight of the line and its intention. The language demonstrates her stumbling steps toward the rest of her life, and my own gasping breath at the thought of it.

I did not make for myself a "no multisyllabic words" rule when I set out to write about this. On the other hand, I did decide to force the issue at hand by ending ten or eleven consecutive lines in the poem "In" (page 69) with a word containing an "in"-like sound. What poets strive for in drafting a poem is such an intense internal focus, bolstered by all they've internalized about the craft of poetry, that they are disposed to make the poem look and sound right in the context of itself; what they must strive for in revision is to examine closely what they've now got for material, asking whether it produces the best effect on every level they can imagine, and to push it around accordingly. Often writers work long and hard before they are satisfied that the poem appears to have simply "come out that way"—all aligned for the melding of form, music, and content. An educated reader is the judge of how satisfactorily this gets accomplished.

This doesn't mean that everything has to fit perfectly into some predetermined mold, or that I (to get more personal) will not occasionally miss an opportunity to improve a word or phrase, but that overall there is an intricate weave just tight enough to form an artful, affecting whole.

"In" (page 69) is about an actual place, a huge Guatemalan field of quicksand covered in grass. It is such an unfamiliar site (or sight) that, even though the first three and a half stanzas (the first half of the seven-stanza poem) are mere description of it, it still feels like it must be a metaphor for something. Try to read it purely as description, and if metaphorical suggestions come to you, you can let them in. In reading, as in writing, it's generally a good idea to start from a stance of solid ground, from which you might be moved to another level, rather than immediately jumping into either ether or muck.

In

We lay down these pathways, long planks, as bridges
across the force of gravity. This field
looks like a smooth field of grass—too smooth,
we notice—and no cows graze on it. Their skeletons,
we are told, swim heavily down below.

In the land of earthquake, volcano, and this quicksand,
we move cautiously. This long, pretty lawn, cleared
mysteriously from the craggy rocks and woods,
is a mud as thick as mercury, a flood
of solid earth. Step on and you step in.

If you walk out on the board that takes your weight,
stamp down on the splintering wood, you see waves
buckling the acreage, and feel the friction of your shoes
shifting over your feet. The whole dictionary of earth,
air to zenith, liquid to solid, embraces this strangest place.

It smells of honey and creosote, something thickening,
unclear. What lingers or hesitates down there,
invisible or forgotten?
Depths resonate, depths sing and call
for sinking down, for falling in, for overwhelm. Depths sound

a dreadful music in minor key, a beckoning.
I shake the long plank. This emerald meadow is so tempting,
such an invitation to immerse. Something
powerful wants me, something that says: Fall in.
And feel the softness of this moist soil soothe your skin:

Let it in.
I want to risk it, to see if I can dive in, even swim,
to see if I can work with it, artist and medium.
Let me see how long I can hold my breath in,
tight and hard and swelling against my bones,

so it takes the shape of that room inside those walls
outside of which flow the quicksand and the overarching
bowl of sky. And when the time comes to let burst
that breath, like an earthquake to let it asunder.
I will swallow the wine of this steepened earth.

In this case, the place itself inspired in me the sensations now in the poem—wonder so extreme it compels you to eschew caution and enter an element that's sure to kill you. Once the temptation takes hold, those repeated line-endings of "in" sounds serve as a subtle but insistent finger beckoning. It's possible this poem could be interpreted alternatively as a call to immersion and letting go, an invitation from the devil, or perhaps simply a fantasy during an otherworldly moment on earth. I hope when it is time for me to go I will give myself over to the experience as wholeheartedly as I said I would in the imaginary, cathartic world of the poem but managed to refrain from doing in that actual, eerie place.

Sound plays an integral role in "The Wind Is" (page 72), a love poem that animates the air between the speaker and the distant lover.

The Wind Is

The wind is a field, a force
of habit in the world.
No roads, no markers,
no destinations. All it wants

is to travel. By turns it unravels,
a dusty blanket, a freshly peeled
pear left out to dry.

The wind is an heir, a far
cry from home. Given, given.
An indifferent owner. In its carriage

fly the looselimbed, the unnatural
vagabond birds in flight.

I've stood out there waiting: Lift me,
take me, I have somewhere
to go. It passes, passes, listing
east and west, the turning points
of the compass. Listening,

I've heard your sigh across the brightened
miles as if no one
and nothing moved between.

Instead of using conventional end-rhyme, the poem's rhythms of repeated sound are syncopated, constantly returning to previous sounds and tweaking familiar expressions ("force of habit," "a far cry") into new contexts, as if following the twists and turns of actual wind gusts. In addition, ending the first line on "force" creates interplay with "field"—the wind is a forcefield = impenetrable—and also stresses the word "force"—wind is a force—so that adding to the sentence with the prepositional clause ("of habit") in the next line then shifts the sense of "force," in the way we noticed when we talked about lines in Step 1. A similar series of possibilities happens later in the poem with the line ending "far."

Now you follow: The "a" of "habit" returns in "travel" which in turn gets rhymed by "unravels." In between, we get the shorter "a" of "marker" and "wants." Next, the "f"s of "freshly" and "left"—with their vowel rhyme (called assonance)—echo those of "freed" and "force." We move on to "p"s in "peeled" and "pear," and "pear" gets a rhyme in "heir" which is a play, of course, on "air" (and also contributes to the sense of "given"). Then we get nine short "i"s starting with "wind" in line 8 and going through "lift" in line 13. Later the twirling "s"s enter like brushing leaves or dust, and in the last stanza the four long "i"s stretch the time and distance apart.

Most of these are airy, or whistling, windy sounds; "f"s and "p"s are less open than "s"s and vowels, but they too require wind and pressure in the mouth to pronounce. The title becomes not just the first three words but the focus of the poem, and finally is the "answer" to the suggested question at the end: "What moves between us?" Nothing but wind comes between us—but look at how alive that wind is, not an empty thing at all. Even so, even with all that, I can still hear your small sigh. Ah, love.

And all this "surface texture" doesn't even address what the words are saying, in terms of mental messages. I could go into that too, but maybe, knowing all you now do about the messages of its sounds and rhythms, and how the abstractions implied in the poem (air, love, distance) become concretized by all these auditory "facts," you are now ready to read more deeply into the actual words of the poem and find what else is going on.

But don't get too bogged down in it. Accept that some words or phrases will more readily yield to you than others, and some choices, like that pear, may be purely for the ear and could just as well have been apples and oranges. Except that wouldn't have sounded as good.

Home (Angel)

Now that you
                are asleep
I lean far out the window
         on this   the ground floor
              of heaven
and there is no
        sound
                in the infinite
shades of darkness
        save the clouds
stepping lightly over the leaves
      and the insects
                  keening
      in thin air
like blood thrilling
                in the inner ear
of night—
      all those tender wings
slipping through spaces   lately
   left open
             by your laughter.

Walking through the Ice Storm

I'll admit I was scared,
but not of falling
on the frozen road. It was you
who mostly missed the ground.
If I held on to you
it was not from fear
but so you'd have something
to stay for, to believe in.
I listened to the bitter air
hissing, flinging its blistered
beads, sharp as syllables:
Luck. Fate. Bullets.
A sky of ice fell over
everything we said, encased it
in glass caskets. I said
you use your loneliness to wound me.
You said your kindness
poisons me. I felt the sky
cut into slender nails
slipping through my skin.
I heard the cold November trees
grieving like hooded widows.
I saw you gliding beside me
like the ghost not yet
cold enough for this storm
to bury.

Step 4

⚜ IMAGES ⚜

Poems Can Make You See Things That Aren't There

SO FAR WE'VE looked at what we see right on the page—the concrete elements, like a poem's shape, that "spell out" the abstract subject of a poem—and we've also broken things down into bits and pieces. Now let's stand back and see the big picture.

Words and alphabets themselves were once pictures (some still are), and even now, when presented with a word, we see instead a thing. We do this all the time: Tree. Mother. Boat. And we name things after what they look like: Mouse. Did you picture your computer tool or the little animal? We use words to spell out, or "paint," pictures of things. William Blake called imagery the "Foundation of the Sublime." In fact it is not only the representation of sight but of all senses.

The power of image is colossal. We all have experienced how an image conjured from our lives—of a person, place, thing or scenario—has the ability to completely change our mood, even our pulse. "A dagger of the mind" (Macbeth) does almost as much violence as a dagger in hand; sometimes it's hard to tell the two apart.

Not all poems employ images; some consist of nothing but. In most of the poems here, I use a combination of "showing" and "telling," like most films, which move from scene to scene but include talking as well.

"A dagger of the mind" (Macbeth) does almost as much violence as a dagger in hand.

Among poetry's images—words that describe what we can visualize or otherwise sense—you'll find a variety of offerings, including ones that are immediately recognizable from our experience of living here on planet Earth and ones that may be metaphors or more unfamiliar ways of describing. Because you're human, your amazing brain is going to go to work for you; imagining (imaging) is a process that comes naturally.

Let's start with "The Gardener" (page 79), because it uses words to depict the same things that the painting after which it's named illustrates—an interaction between a man and a woman, with several others in interested attendance, and the suggestion of possible relationships between them. (You might be able to locate the actual understated but tender-hearted piece itself in a collection of Baroque art.)

The Gardener

After the painting by M. Le Nain, c. 1655

In standing just beyond her skirts,
in leaning in, and
in that shy lift
of your little finger on the handle
of your hoe—in these we know you.

And she must look up soon,
accept this rose you hold for her.

You leave your eyes on the sure
distance between your finger and the tip
of hers which touches one petal
as if testing it for texture.

One child peers up from under
these splendid hands suspended
like other buds
in all the dark surrounding.

The fall of cloth, the long
pause of women and girls, all
tilt us toward your sweet intent.

Your red coat's sleeve is torn.
She will never mend it, nor mention
what you did today. You will tend
to your garden, she to the table, where
she'll slice the whitest parsnips.

Almost everything in this poem faithfully describes the scene, but that doesn't mean it's not being subjectively interpreted. A little adjective like "shy" to point attention to that raised pinky has the power to sway your view of this gardener. Is the recipient of the rose the woman of the house on whose approval the gardener's livelihood depends, or is she one of the kitchen maids, the one the gardener loves? Are the servants permitted romance? There's fictionalizing here, as what do I know of the fate of that tear in his sleeve, let alone whether they'll manage marriage or a private tryst? Just as the words allow the scene to be "seen" into, the painting conveys more than meets the eye, an emotional content that makes the viewer feel yearning and tension, sympathy and hope.

In poetry, as in all art, conversation, and even thought, detail is the indicator of what matters most. The direction and proximity of our focus tell us the degree of importance, as when a film camera zooms in on a face or your friend talks your ear off for half an hour about her new boyfriend. Poems often alternate between close-ups and panning, tightening and loosening the reins on our perspective and thoughts.

"Something Left Out in the Rain" (page 81) begins with a medium-range scene in which the speaker gets out of bed in the night to stand at the rain-streaked window.

Something Left Out in the Rain

When I sleep in strange houses and it rains,
I rise up from my bed and stare,
bewildered, out the dark twilled windows.
There's something left out in the rain,
I say, but I can't remember what it is.
Something in my memory rusts or shines
or sinks into the earth,
lost now, but still of great importance.
A baseball glove, a shoe, a book or a tool,
a gift, once upon a time, owned
and forgotten. But more than this,
some ancestral awe of water. Floods.
Lost land. Precarious shelter. The rain
spins off the leaves of trees, the bark,
corners of strangers' homes and barns.
Or slides down the rails and steps
of fire escapes, dark as spears.
The axe? The fenceposts? What?
What is it that worries me, half-recalled
from another life? Something long ago familiar
about the grasses drenched in risen drops,
the sparrows stretching dry their wings,
insects emerging from between cleaned stones,
the ancient rains that made them.
I don't know what it is at the eroding edge of mind
that sticks there like a summer-swollen door;
but the rain stops, and while I sleep,
the wet world evaporates in slow inaudible sighs.

Once we're introduced to the opening circumstances of the poem, reader's and speaker's minds range over the same images—small, specific items that could have been left outside: "a baseball glove, a shoe, a book or a tool." Not being able to know for sure tinges the images with a slight sense of worry and loss, because what "rusts or shines / or sinks into the earth" is not only out in the rain but "in my memory."

And then in the twelfth line we suddenly have zoomed outward into a long, collective (un)conscious view: "Ancestral awe of water. Floods. / Lost land. Precarious shelter." Primal panic—and then a return to more familiar things nearer at hand, though we are not entirely released from past lives, since the rain sliding off buildings is "dark as spears." Squinting even more closely at blades of grass, "risen drops," sparrows, and even insects between stones, we're between a rock and a hard place ourselves—in the worlds of both present and prehistoric past, where we are reminded that it was "ancient rains" that formed these very stones eons ago.

We never put our finger on just what that thing left out in the rain was; we can't solve that mystery because the sensation that disturbed the speaker in this rain and strange place goes so much farther back in her animal presence on Earth than memory itself can say. The speaker finally sleeps again while the forces of time and elements continue on as they always have, and those "slow, inaudible sighs," if not the world's, are probably really hers.

An undulating range of images, combined with ideas, can flow through our minds as well as our emotions; sometimes the two work in tandem. "Blue" (page 84) presents a challenge, as it uses less image altogether, and what there is is less familiar than a shoe or a fencepost.

Step 4
IMAGES

Blue

"Man worries; God laughs."
—YIDDISH PROVERB

Blue is given to nothing
to save it from being invisible.
What is the indiscernible, lovely line
between air and sky?
Real, but as if imaginary,
that moment of blue is the awe-
filled air, sometimes called heaven,
the vanishing point forever
fading out
so as not to seem too sudden.
The unseen and the brilliant there
are one.
Where the future passes on
and spring overtakes the snow,
is all that is known
of the true home of that hue.
There is no one single
glimpse of grace to learn
why, or where, the sky is blue, beyond
the shadow of a doubt.
God lives in that place, laughing.

"The unseen and the brilliant . . . / are one" is a kind of Zen koan. You have to work harder internally, asking your thinking mind to get involved, to see a thing not really concretely visible—the color blue tinting air and "defining" heaven—or else let go of mental reasoning altogether. The poem asks you to imagine, perhaps on faith alone, things in time and space before they even become experiential—a change of season, the future becoming the past—and in the end the metaphysical exercise, like many metaphysical exercises that captivate us, is unanswerable, and even absurd.

A poem, then, formulates its own inner "logic" or truth, and if you want to read it for what it is, and not for its scientific linear provability, you have to suspend not only belief but normal logic. Don't dismiss a poem just because it doesn't "make sense." A lot of important sense is made in just this oblique way, or as the poet Charles Simic once said, combining the abstract with a nice concrete image, "There is truth with eyes open and truth with eyes closed and the two don't always recognize each other on the street."

Through imagery, poems make things happen that can't "really" happen. When you read a poem with these sensory data, whether or not it quite succeeds, your mind makes the effort to make sense of them.

In "Still Life with Woman" (page 87), after some easier descriptions of a vegetable and a kitchen tool held in the woman's hand, we get this: "On countertops, window-sills, patience piles up / like . . . dust." Patience is not a concrete thing; you can't see patience, though you might see indicators of it such as facial expressions or gestures, but nevertheless there it is on countertops and window-sills, and the mind goes right along with the strangeness of it, simply making patience look like dust—or, in other words, letting dust, which takes a lot of time to gather, represent (present anew) patience. We take metaphors like silk takes dye.

Still Life with Woman

In every room there is a woman, palpable.
She takes object lessons from the inanimate.
In the scene, she holds a large red pepper, its skin
taut over muscle and a secret, subdued core.

She has shaken it like a child's rattle,
and now contemplates its reticence. Her knife,
a fine tool, lusts for the chance to split
its shining stillness, its infinitude.

On countertops, windowsills, patience piles up
like the sweet dust of mourning and time past.
Shadows spread from under coffee cups,
stopping short of overflow, the way voices

reach in toward her, dissolve unheard.
She is like vegetables, like china, smooth, clean,
unconscious of the myths of tableware, fables
of toys, studies of form and change and form.

What does she feel? She feels red pepper,
paring knife, chance. The way she is actually
poised in the midst of things:
wood, glass, light from above, this life.

In "Instead" (page 94) I ask you to visualize all kinds of things we don't usually see—because that's what the poem is about. Maybe dragonflies don't really see "the throb in the throat / of humidity" either—if humidity even has a throat, which would anthropomorphize it— but the extremity of the thought and the effort it takes to make what we can of it—to imagine it—accentuate the gulf between insect and human eyesight. (And if we could see such a thing—wouldn't that be cool?)

In the poetic technique called "imagism," images constitute the entire poem, uninterpreted and unencumbered by connectors. These images are loaded; they speak to our senses as well as our thoughts, embodying ideas and meaning, not necessarily explaining or pointing out the way to these connections.

Playing with imagery in another way, "Conspiracy" (page 96) projects images of metaphors and even synesthesia, or the combining of senses, to intensify matters, as in "listening for the crack / of light from under closed doors" which requires "crack" to be both a sound and a sight (another example of the surprises possible with enjambment and multiple meaning). The poem's world of abandonment makes everything suspect. Even the logs in the fire, with their double use of the word "pitch," have seen better days. I love that our language lets us use words in so many transmutable forms, so that we see and then see again, as in the line in "The Hoe" (page 97): "puddles and floods." Following the word "water," they take shape as representations of water, in noun form. But then the next line reveals them to be verbs; "puddles" and "floods" are not things but actions. Having already visualized them as fixed nouns, we now have to shift our minds to visualize them in time.

In "This Time" (page 90) are "aging" and "browning" adjectives that describe the nouns following them, or are they verbs—processes that the deer's movements make happen to the fences and the leaves—or are they both? That deer is sometimes so utterly still that she alters her surroundings by proxy; her stillness is so extreme, the poem tells us, it becomes an image that seems to move the inanimate: "Each time the deer stops, / rocks roam freely in the field." Then with the deer's next motion she "redefines" the landscape, as if the objects in the field were playing Freeze Tag with her. All this may simply be poetic license, or exaggeration used for effect (which in literature is called "hyperbole"), but while the poem's claims may seem "illogical," nature has in fact done stranger things.

This Time

Still frame. The deer
is a presence
like spring, like fall,
unprecedented.

The deer moves like trees move
in storms: of necessity,
heavy with grace, somewhere
between forever and a moment.

Her head swings slowly
like time, forward and back.
Then, stillness—a flattening
of dimension, a sudden sepia.

Now the deer shifts
to life, bends her neck
to windfall, lifts to fruit
left on limbs.

Each time the deer stops,
rocks roam freely in the field.
Each move redefines—revives—
the landscape: aging fences,

browning leaves, the brittle
perennial reach of weeds,
just as each day
tomorrow is renamed.

But the deer's pauses,
made of listening,
bathed in patience, are tools
that sculpt surrounding space,

meant to lead us to dusting
leaves, moss growing
on stones, the flit
of our own lashes.

Now she looks right at us,
we think she sees us
but her evening ritual
continues, careful,

a tension acutely becalmed.
Deer, those apples are free.
Our breath etches the glass,
our eyes sting

from the effort not to blink,
not to let go this time.
The deer stands as if ascending,
as if always, as if casually

poised to leap.

A poem's words and pictures shifting in place like this play with our perceptions like an Escher print's progression of overlapping, interwoven, images. They are anamorphic, meaning not so much shapeshifters as things that have the power to transform themselves at the same time that they remain what they are.

While poems laden with image upon image without explanatory "talk" can come across as coherent, relay a feeling through their pictures, or seem to tell a segment of story, some may mimic the sudden, disjointed cuts from scene to scene we know from dreams.

Art often likes to order aspects of life that we, sometimes just below the surface of our consciousness, fear are random—coincidence, "unfair" losses, even good luck. In contrast, some collage techniques (in any medium, including poetry), perhaps with antecedents in Surrealism, refuse to play to our hopes that life's series of happenstances will reveal instructive meaning if only we think positively enough.

Just as some of us relish ascribing to the omitted links and separate snapshots of our dreams interpretation and meaning while others are bored by the thought, we also bring our personal inclinations to this kind of poetry. Whether you're fond of the work of sense-making or not, you are wired to know, instinctively, archetypically, how important images are. The subliminal charge of trying to discover (or invent) meaning may feel to some of us like a waste of our busy time, but it excites sparks of intriguing possibility in others.

When I collage words, phrases, ideas or images to

make a poem, I enjoy the process of connecting (most, not all) the dots, finding or creating the "glue" that can bind them into a new whole. Metaphor is a mystical math that says 1+1=1. Galway Kinnell has instructed us that making metaphors is the moral way to go. When we juxtapose disparate things to reveal their formerly unearthed connections, we see in a new light their unity, and can actually visualize—*sense*—the abstract. Robert Frost suggested, even more elementally, that this is our most fundamental system of learning. Certainly we feel an awakening when formerly unexposed connections are revealed to us, or when a feeling is animated by means of metaphor or image. When we say, "Oh, I see!" or "I hear you," we have embodied—incorporated—meaning.

When the abstractions implied in poetry's concrete structure, words and sound are *realized*—made perceptible—by images, our minds will do almost anything to internalize their representations, and once we have, emotions are quick to follow.

Instead

Where I see nothing instead
 the dragonfly sees its own flight,
  the waves its wings
   throw through the atmosphere
above the pond. June. Sunlight
 jewels its thirty thousand eyes,
  whole worlds possible
   in each one. The dragonfly
seizes the air, every molecule
 an object of mercy or reckoning.
  Water seethes in the air's embrace,
   condensing, evaporating,
between pond and sky,
 between eye and eye.
  The dragonfly—mythical, simple,
   weightless Pegasus—
sees the throb in the throat
 of humidity, the expansion
  of atoms, suspension bridges
   spanning every hue.
Think of the refraction!
 Think of prisms, how the dragonfly
  hovers between rays thick as mirrors,
   conspicuous as neon—
finds its path through forests
 invisible to me, in one square inch
  of light—witnesses the air
   as it flies up into futures

blue or cloud, or falls
    back to the pond, still cold from the spring.
      The dragonfly rides the train
        of tomorrow's rain
down the rails to a taste of blackfly.
    The waltz, the hunt, the loom,
      the dragonfly's ancestral dance
        and the weave
of actual time and physical space.
    There is so much that I don't know.
      The dragonfly knows ash and dust,
        pollen, insect, seed and scent,
light, lightness, shadow, shape,
    the lift and swoop and race of wings,
      last year's disintegration,
        next century's tree. Tonight
I could look up into a summer's night
    and see there this life
      before it existed, and after,
        and instead.

Conspiracy

I lie awake all night
listening to the dust
murmuring under furniture,
listening for the crack
of light from under closed doors,
hearing the sere heat
in the pipes, the rise and fall
of water in the drains.
There is the sound of my sleep
turning back, taking
all the necessary silence
elsewhere. All night
the brittle bray of logs
in the fire, the high pitch
of their sudden memories
of green.
I listen for the shudder
of window panes
breaking free of splintered frames,
hear the stirrings
among the pillow's feathers
as they try to fly again
and in the curtains closed in vain
against the call of day.
Now the lonely sound
of someone breathing,
a heart beating in my own body,
the nails ripping
out from the fingers
as if they too are leaving
for a better home.

The Hoe

In March the earth breaks open, stirs
from its suspension: water
puddles and floods
our road. You take your hoe
when we go walking, and you fold
soaked earth into soft pleats,
to let the water flow. You free
the orphaned pools to travel and rejoin
their brooks and streams,
and the braided water leaps
between new wet walls, and falls
over the edges of road
and into woods.
With your hoe you scoop
sodden leaves into woven wells, so
these floodgates open, this drawbridge unlocks,
these little excesses of ice and rain and snow
run off, without turning back.
I stay, and watch you clear our way,
parting mud with sure true strokes,
leading water to where it wanted to go.

Step 5

⚘ EMOTION ⚘

Poems Can Make You Feel Things

I ONCE READ the words of a former slave. Writing about a time before he had learned to read and write, when he heard a white man read aloud from a book, he described his wonder at the strange voice that came through from the book, as if a secret being resided there. When the reader left, the listener picked up the book and gazed at the pages with expectation, but try as he might, he could not find any voice that would speak to him. He said he felt that even in this he was shunned and shrunken as a person, as he had been all his life as a slave.

It is a strange and beautiful thing that little inky squiggles on a plain ground can speak to us. Don't take it for granted. When they do, we might laugh out loud in

It is a strange and beautiful thing that little inky squiggles on a plain ground can speak to us.

⚘ 99

the middle of a crowded subway, oblivious to witnesses, or fear so much for a character's fate we miss our stop. That another person's life can translate so profoundly into ours, over the vastness of time and space, through the act of reading, is one of the most life-affirming gifts I know, especially in that it depends not so much on any individual experience in age, place or happenstance as on our more primally shared needs, hopes and fears as mortal guests on this planet—and the powerful magic of written language.

One of my children, when I read to him, used to cup his hands along the page and "scoop up" the words to hold them tight against his chest. Another had to stop reading books at bedtime for several years because the sadness he felt when the characters suffered was so intense he couldn't sleep—although he chose sad stories because they affirmed and even comforted something dark in himself. And, even before she had learned to read, my youngest child slept best when she was accompanied in her bed by so many books she couldn't turn over without clonking an elbow or her head on one.

Though I am sitting at my desk, listening to Bach while my now teenage children are all at school, writing these words revives the images of these decade-old memories and makes my throat constrict. If I were just skimming over the thoughts and not really focusing my full attention on them, as will be the case when I proofread the same words, that wouldn't happen. We feel the same meeting of emotions when we fully take in another's words and digest them. It is a recipe depending upon one part ingredients, one part tasting, and one part skill.

The ingredients of a poem that can make you feel things include both what the writer felt and what the writer wrote. But the feeling or ability on the part of the writer won't be as complete as it could be in that poem if a good reader never shows up to savor the results. The reader's participation in completing the work of the writer is the "add water and stir" instruction of frozen concentrate—or, to change metaphors, it is what takes the dormant seed of the poem and plants it so it can grow.

So the reader must give of himself if he wants to get all he can from a poem; it isn't only the writing but the reading as well that takes willingness and skill. If you're reading this, you already have most of what it takes. To take a poem to heart, just as in any encounter with another consciousness, you don't necessarily have to have a lot of specialized knowledge, just the basics—but what you should have is openness.

So let's see what you notice coming in, and how it gets through.

In Walt Whitman's epic poem, "Out of the Cradle Endlessly Rocking," the first sentence is twenty-two lines long. Its subject, "I," shows up in line twenty, and its verb—that necessary, settling, satisfying note in time—only arrives as the very last word.

Out of the cradle endlessly rocking,
Out of the mocking-bird's throat, the musical shuttle,
Out of the Ninth-month midnight,

The feeling or ability on the part of the writer won't be as complete as it could be in that poem if a good reader never shows up to savor the results.

Over the sterile sands and the fields beyond, where the child
leaving his bed
wander'd alone, bareheaded, barefoot,
Down from the shower'd halo,
Up from the mystic play of shadows twining and twisting as
if they were alive,
Out from the patches of briers and blackberries,
From the memories of the bird that chanted to me,
From your memories, sad brother, from the fitful risings and
fallings I heard
From under that yellow half-moon late-risen and swollen as
if with tears,
From those beginning notes of yearning and love there
in the mist,
From the thousand responses of my heart never to cease,
From the myriad thence-arous'd words,
From the word stronger and more delicious than any,
From such as now they start the scene revisiting,
As a flock, twittering, rising, or overhead passing,
Borne hither, ere all eludes me, hurriedly,
A man, yet by these tears a little boy again,
Throwing myself on the sand, confronting the waves,
I, chanter of pains and joys, uniter of here and hereafter,
Taking all hints to use them, but swiftly leaping
beyond them,
A reminiscence sing.

This construction itself, of delayed subject or verb
following subclause after subclause and reversed syntax
("I . . . a reminiscence sing") causes so much tension
that a reader is already immersed in rhythm and feeling
before she even knows what's going on and to whom or
by whom it is happening. Carl Phillips is a contemporary
poet who makes wonderful use of the technique. When

you're reading a poem like that, you're swept along in suspense and anticipation. Those are emotions.

Even delaying the subject and action by one or two phrases can be more interesting than sentence after sentence of noun-verb, noun-verb. "Home (Angel)" (Step 3, page 75) is a small poem made up of one sentence whose informational center is in line three: "I lean . . . out the window." The opening lines give a context and a bit of setting, and as you go on you can hear the summer insects defining the night's silence in all those "s," "th," "v" and "f" sounds. If this person is leaning way out the window after someone else has fallen asleep, something—I'll let you guess—has probably happened that involves a feeling; in this poem, it's a joyous one. We may be in bed here, but it's "the ground floor / of heaven." Participial (-ing) verbs, which are in continuous, not finished, time, like "keening," "thrilling," and "slipping," along with the breathless skipping of the lines, describe the charged atmosphere of love.

Many poems come right out and name their predominant feelings, or at least talk about them directly, with the speaker of the poem expressing what she felt. "Grief" (page 116) is, well, about grief. Some poems use images to illustrate how someone feels, as in "Conspiracy" (Step 4, page 96), and others, such as "Walking through the Ice Storm" (Step 3, page 76), choose words (". . . bitter air / hissing, flinging its blistered / beads, sharp as syllables") that will influence a reader by their sound, force, and associations. In these cases, neither the poem nor its speaker is telling you what to feel. Instead, you're offered clues which stir your own feelings, which you add to the mix, in this way engaging you so you project what you already have inside.

You are adept enough at reading a poem now that you can allow this process to occur. Rather than leading you through poems, pretending to be able to tell you what they make you feel, I will instead say a bit about what I felt as I created some of them and what I hope they carry with them. I suggest you read them first, though, so what I say is less introduction and more postscript, with your own reactions to them the main event. When you come to the poems, just remember what you've learned about letting poems wash through you, and stay open.

Themes of poetry everywhere have always related to how best to live, such as by connecting to the Other—animal, vegetable or mineral—or by overcoming loneliness, separation, disagreeable politics and societal situations, violence, poverty and other hardships, as well as by questioning, learning, growing, and celebrating all the felicities that make life easier, and how to reckon with death. These are themes of life—and you know poetry is full of life.

These are
themes of life—
and you know
poetry is full
of life.

When I think of my poems, or more importantly my urge to write poems, I can identify two or three predominant areas of emotion, which fall under the above categories and which I hope you too will find and feel there.

The first I'll address, under the category of "how best to live," is perfectly simple (well, sometimes): Love. Love of partner, family, children, food, home, body, nature, seasons, plants, weather. In sum, thanks. In the general canon of the ages, we have tended to think of love poems as being addressed to a "you" or to a spiritual presence in a writer's life, but experiences or visions beheld can cause their variations of love as well, including wonder, celebration, excitement, awe, prayerfulness, or gratitude.

The Nelson Bog

There never was a thing so crystalline and colorless,
steeped in every form and shade
of a single element called silver gray.

Twilight at any time of day: say afternoon,
say March, a warming trend close down below the air.

The bog loomed like fantasy—the water silver gray,
the ice, silver gray, floating along surfaces—
the only horizon between water and silver gray sky.

The sky hanging like wet moss in densest mists
over steaming ice, and reflected—below, above, within
the water—a silver gray wave of air like smoke

diffusing the diffused.
And finally, brush-stroked, the trees

a silver gray more darkly impenetrable,
less lightly mirrored, rising up from a fog like parishioners
too moved to speak their prayers.

"Nelson Bog" aims to embody the worshipful, quiet awe I felt when I saw it, which is finally stated through the comparison at the end to churchgoers. "Ripening" (page 108) is one in a seemingly unstoppable series of poems I write about picking blueberries. There is something so exquisite about finding food—especially sweet blue food—outside in the wild, I am overcome with love every time.

Ripening

Nothing but time—when it is time—
can make the blueberries ripe, their skins
plush as lips, deeply filled with the colors
of bruise and breath and bliss.

Nothing can rush this, this slow swell
of growth, this lush and lavish splash
of fruit, this bloom and blush and burst.
You can't feed it anything to speed its time—

nothing generosity or economy, hope or desire can do.
What softens them is all that, too, can soften you:
the length of days spun by the wheel of sun and moon
the same way one continuous thread becomes a cloth.

Like the reviving trees in spring, or astonished flowers
emerging from unfrozen ground, these blueberries
feed on light. Light is their cue and key, the same thing
that feeds me what I know and do not yet know but will.

Because I eat blueberries in midsummer, I like age,
the news it brings of things I've known well all along.
I like the questions it poses, and the slow
but sudden way it replies. All the while

I have been too busy to wait, I have been waiting
for this, and this, and this: each successive,
deliberate day. Through the wild plenty of time,
nature's pace is a walk, a mild ramble

over mountainsides and fields. Who remembers berries
in November? I want to forget nothing, miss nothing,
but then—the trees fall away in windblown, broken strokes
and let in newer light, and there is still more to behold.

Now, all summer, we have been patient and excited,
almost a year since we climbed our home's hills with our fingers
combing the green for its deep-sea blue. Here, the blueberries
will ripen in the third week of July, no sooner—not even

if cities are built in a day, or swords are beaten
into plowshares. There's no hurry, no hurrying them.
And when they come, after the solstice, after the fireworks,
after all, I will roll each one in my hands,

name them, and count them each like blessings.
Then with my tongue I will parse and split and swallow them
so they enter the bloodstream all red and blue because now
is the only time.

While the bog poem is a fairly closed evocative image, about a bog, this blueberry one isn't really about blueberries—or isn't only about blueberries; it describes blueberries in terms of time, which means it also refers to aging. The poem connects the act of eating off the ripened bushes when we can with the contingencies of time's other aspects in our lives, and instead of resisting those not-always loved influences of time, I am inspired or taught by nature to accept and even appreciate them. Not always, but we'll get to that.

Love is often shaded by the pain of loss, or at least the knowledge that what is loved can be lost, and this overlap of life and death is another area of poetry, perhaps the most vast. Shakespeare expresses it peerlessly in his Sonnet LXIV:

> Ruin has taught me thus to ruminate,
> That Time will come and take my lover away.
>> This thought is as a death, which cannot choose
>> But weep to have that which it fears to lose.

Shakespeare may have nailed it, but that doesn't mean the rest of us won't keep trying to say it again, our own ways. In "Grief" (page 116) I put it this way: love is "the leaven of all sorrow." Mexican poet Octavio Paz has said, "To love is to die / and live again and die again. . . ." Like most people, sometimes I can be philosophical about this truth and other times I find it hard to accept.

Like centuries of poets before, in a large percentage of my poems I balance on the precarious brink between the happiness of loving and the fear or pain of losing, and sometimes the best that can be is a place of

Shakespeare may have nailed it, but that doesn't mean the rest of us won't keep trying to say it again, our own ways.

wistfulness, which I suppose is just a kind of truce some-where between war and peace (two other big subjects in poetry). Poet Wesley McNair advises that the poems that most affect us are those whose emotions are complex. And how could it not be so? The other extreme is a greeting card. Or as singer John Gorka says of life's troubles, "Too much and you're not portable; not enough and you'll be making happy rhymes."

No matter the matter, as readers we physically experience our own emotions in an empathic dynamic between all we bring with us and all the poem embodies. A poem can convey its crucial triggers in many ways, including line lengths, awkward or spurring breaks and pauses, shifting or dead-on tones, relentless or opposing associations within words and images, and strong descriptions of a personally identifiable character's plight. The tension of a poem's simultaneous or alternating conflicting emotions can be particularly affecting, because the more we feel, and the less able we are of easily categorizing or explaining feelings away, the more unable we are to disengage.

Two poems on the "mixed emotion" fence are "Learning to Read" (Step 2, page 58) and "Beholden" (page 112). In the first, the struggle with the grip of time is simply put: In the parent's eyes, whenever a child takes steps toward independence, "every gain of his is my gain / and my loss." The second, "Beholden," acknowledges that it's the very awareness of inevitable end that makes the beloved precious; the present and the knowledge it will become past cannot be disentangled, so we might as well make use of their union, "for balance, unbalancing, uplift."

. . . as readers we physically experience our own emotions in an empathic dynamic between all we bring with us and all the poem embodies.

Beholden

Still I am not sure which is most vivid—
the love now risen from its previous absence,
or the future loss it rides like a shadow,
the eye's after-image of a bright light gone.
In any case, with its harrowing blades,
this fertile line of love already
draws through me a beautiful symmetry:
the invisible, downward reaching of dark and buried roots,
and the opening, airing branches that they mimic.
Always, love is something coming to an end,
something that could die before its time
and so you live in it, a world, a frame,
the borders that define. You memorize it,
day by day, like the lines of the earth's face
mapped and changing, mapped again and again
changing, over centuries, the impossible
becoming true before you. And like that,
you look for the shapes of things now being
that once were not: no matter
how you hold a day, it sets into the year,
buried, lost. In memory its sheen
is another branch. We see that coming.
It is precisely that passage, that change, that tunneling
through the soil of time—that dread—
that makes love what it is: so rich, so far
beside itself with beauty, beholden to it,
because it can never be held.
It's just that love is the highest point, the lightning rod

that draws to it the crooked path of sorrow
which it waits for, depends upon, uses in advance,
not the way that we use air—of necessity, for life—
but, instead, the way that birds use air:
for balance, unbalancing, uplift.

A more single-minded poem is "Permission" (page 118), whose downright terrified resentment (as opposed to that Zen-like acceptance or even joy felt in "Ripening," page 108) at the inevitability of not being able to be returned to life like a newly-rooted cutting is an accusation addressed directly to the plant—which, however, the speaker does have some compassion for; after all, she suspects "this must hurt" and she does go out and bury it so it can "come to life again." Simply stopping to address these issues, of losing one's grip on life either psychologically or mortally, can raise enough complex emotions that poets don't necessarily need to say much more about them. They only need to find the images, language, or avenue of approach that will let us neither avoid nor cure our fear, but safely experience and share it.

How does my brief overview of the weight these poems carry influence what you feel reading them? Does it confirm or confuse your own reaction? For your own experience between you and a poem, read "The Necessity" (in Step 6, page 124). You read it in Step 1 for its shape; this time read it for emotions. What does the lamb feel? How do you know that? Was it because you read the word "anger" in reference to it, or did you already know? And what about the speaker—what does she feel about the lamb, herself, or how to live her life, as she takes in what's going on? What is the strongest feeling *you* come away with from the poem? How did that feeling come to you? Are your feelings mixed, straightforward, new, re-enforced? Do they change as you read the poem subsequent times?

How you answer these questions and others that come to you, possibly not even consciously, as you read, is how you negotiate the terrain of the poem. Some people like paved roads, others wooded trails, and still others just head right off through the undergrowth, bushwacking. Whichever path you take, if you stay aware and keep your senses alert, you'll encounter new and stimulating things, and your journey probably won't turn out exactly the same as anyone else's.

You are half responsible (and fully rewarded) for making emotions in a poem come alive again. If you do share with a poet a specific experience of place, birth, or other granfalloon, your response will perhaps come more readily. But even a poem written by a geisha centuries ago in Japan can open up as much in you as one in which you see a reflection of your current, individual life.

While many other elements of poetry are kin to arts, play, puzzles, problem-solving or primal instinct, this one—emotion—may make demands of a personal, psycho-social or even psychological kind. Successful interaction with poems (or fiction, for that matter) is rooted as much in learning empathy as literary skills. Perhaps it is because the two are so linked that reading is such a moral and enlightening activity.

Some people like paved roads, others wooded trails, and still others just head right off through the undergrowth, bushwacking.

Grief

I am ashamed as I try to sleep,
counting the wounded and the dead
in this old day's news,

the grieving ones they leave behind.
Counting stones and bullets, averted needs,
the pretty breaths of my family beside me,
counting on a world that I don't trust
to keep my children safe.

What was I thinking? Did I forget those others,
the rubble of their troubled worlds
and mine? Does it fill their days—

their remembering? Or do they remember too
to choose their favorite breakfast bowls,
that red dress, the time to step out of doors?
When I lean my body over the fragile forms
of my husband and children, I am afraid

I am not strong enough to bear
the grief of so much loving, the burden
of our survival from day to day,

or of what we can't live without, but will.
How each of us fends off despair—
that is what we are made of
when all else is dust or luck.
Each stranger's grief is not my grief

but it lies under everything, like ice.
Sometimes I fall through it.
Sometimes I walk achingly.

I am not saying their voices rise
above the hum of comfort here and now.
I'm saying I believe that even sweet blue skies
will break away, leaving nothing
between my eyes and the face of a god

who says, Look down into that dark place,
meet your own shadow there.
Go on, take it, take it on. Grieve:

Go down into the dirt.
I want to have already known its taste.
I want to have swallowed it alive.
If I fall asleep tonight,
If I do not die before I wake,

what will have lifted me back to perfect
that other thing that we call hope
is more love: the leaven of all sorrow.

Permission

Tenuous white tendrils, these new roots, keels
on the stems of pussywillow sticks stuffed into a jar.
I see now that they have balanced you for a time,
in a place, between death and life.
Every week in March I tried to wade through the snow
to bring you home, a sign of spring. Finally in April
I could lift my legs high enough over the field
to steal your little puffs of growth. And now
that I have come to throw you back outside, I find
this new life under water. So you have stood in the window,
inert, at first, like a seed, not dead after all—even sprouting
new body parts, learning to live again.
This must hurt, like the rapid and shooting
growth of babies' soft white bones. And this latency,
this ability to plunge into, to feed on, whatsoever element
will take you, amphibious: Of course I am jealous.
Because yes, I will dig for you yet another home,
on this side of winter this time.
You will be permitted to feel the dirt as it enters,
surrounds, every delicate, raw nerve of root and branch.
You will be allowed to remember the long stems, the family
of stems, the air that supported you, and to forget
the months of still, cool water, necessary and cruel. You
will know the deeps, the buried earth, eat it, and be free
to come to life again.

Letting Go

No wonder he laughs—the ceiling is gone
and opening like song. This is new
and he never pauses or looks back
but crawls off toward edges
wherever they may be.
Ten months, and he's just found that onward feeling—
the falling, flying breach
of being born to spring and bodily motion,
the joy of stepping out of doors,
the quick, iambic, heart-beat two-step
of a breathing body displacing space:
Look at him go, safe at a distance.
Earlier this morning, at my breast,
his concentration was as fixed.
His eyes peered at my close skin as if it too
were infinite.

From him I borrow his oaty, newgrown smell,
his spring-rain skin, his cool-water taste.
His mouth is a warm, strong place
where words are yet unborn.
When he is full, he shifts backward
and a line like a spider's silk
blooms between my breast and his lips.
It is beaded with the diluted
saliva'd milk in his mouth.
Wet thread, as clear and strong as the water
of waterfalls, it changes me like waterfalls
change the rocks they travel by. I watch it lengthen,

this waterfall, this web, this thread of life
between us. I hold him—and my breath—
both dearly, and I tell him without words:
This is how I love you, this is how that love
trembles with its tiny musical notes—pearls
of our bodies; this is the warp and weft
that weave you to me loosely, the gravity
that never releases us even when we let go.
This is the embrace that holds as lightly as the sky.
He is listening. I carry him outside.

Step 6
🜊 THOUGHTS 🜊

Poems Can Make You Think

I DON'T JUST mean that poems make you think "what on earth is this poem about?" I mean they make you think (and rethink) about ideas—particularly your own.

Whenever we read, we check ourselves against the opinions and biases of the characters—or authors—we identify with. So we may find ourselves internally nodding in agreement, realizing or validating our views, or we may strike up an argument, articulating opposition. Either way, we examine ourselves and others in the process, and you know that "the unexamined life is not worth living." I used to be one of those truly interactive readers who decorated books' margins with passionate pencilings, starring and underlining everything I thought wise or well said, or exclaiming "NO!" in indignant caps whenever I judged things misguided—as if I were in deep conversation with "real" or at least present people.

I don't need to use a pencil in order to read anymore, but I still enter the world of literature with the expectation of being mentally stimulated in addition to being emotionally moved. Poetry is no exception.

Nonwriters often want to know, "Where do you get your ideas?" Maybe the word "idea" is not the most accurate one for this question; in any case, the almost non-answery answer is life, the whole package. Everything we do and see and hear and read, or imagine. And what do writers mean when they say they have an "idea" for a poem—not that we necessarily would say that? Do we start with an abstract theme or a concrete image, an experience or memory we want to spend some time thinking about, a word or phrase that intrigues or tickles us, an indefinable urge, or what?

All of the above, including the "what." Sometimes we sit down to write without an "idea" in our heads and just see what happens. But if we want to write about an image, experience or memory, it will be more affecting if it contains emotional and/or intellectual stimulants, however understated, and if we want to write about a feeling or thought, we're probably going to need something solid to hold it in, the way water needs a container to take shape and not spill all over the place.

All of the
above,
including the
"what."

"The Necessity" (page 124), mentioned in Step 1 for its shape and read in Step 5 for emotions, is a political poem about anger. I didn't say to myself, I'm going to write about anger. If I had, which is entirely possible, I would have waited—pen poised or while going about my busy life for days—to receive a vehicle for that idea. In this case, I got the vehicle—the "story"—first.

Step 6
THOUGHTS

The Necessity

It isn't true about the lambs.
They are not meek,
They are curious and wild,
full of the passion of spring.
They are lovable,
and they are not silent when hungry.

Tonight the last of the triplet lambs
is piercing the quiet with its need.
Its siblings are stronger
and will not let it eat.

I am its keeper, the farmer, its mother.
I will go down to it in the dark,
in the cold barn,
and hold it in my arms.

But it will not lie still—it is not meek.

I will stand in the open doorway
under the weight of watching trees and moon,
and care for it as one of my own.

But it will not love me—it is not meek.

Drink, little one. Take what I can give you.
Tonight the whole world prowls
the perimeters of your life.

Your anger keeps you alive—
it's your only chance.
So I know what I must do
after I have fed you.

I will shape my mouth to the shape
of the sharpest words,
even those bred in silence.

I will impale with words every ear
pressed upon open air.
I will not be meek.

You remind me of the necessity
of having more hope than fear,
and of sounding out terrible names.

I am to cry out loud
like a hungry lamb, cry loud
enough to waken wolves in the night.

No one can be allowed to sleep.

The poem starts by making a living connection to the common "meek as a lamb" simile, rejecting its stereotype as well as the biblical admonition that it is the meek who shall inherit. (Reference to familiar cultural catchphrases lends a poem the weight of accepted thought reconsidered.) There is a real lamb in this poem, and "it is not meek." It is crying, demanding its rights. In the poem, the lamb teaches us how important anger is in the face of injustice, how important it is not to give up but to fight for the fulfillment of basic needs. "Hunger" is both a real and a metaphoric thing, in the poem as in life. It's also significant in the poem that the angry, loud lamb, who "will not love me" even when given what it wants, is nevertheless "lovable." Asking doesn't change that—in fact asking is the only way to survive and become "curious and wild, / full of the passion of spring." All of the ideas here are embedded in the actual—which in itself was the "idea" for the poem.

Thoughts and ideas inform many, if not most, poems, though some are background or subtle sensibility while others are of central or topical importance. "Beholden" (Step 5, page 112) discusses love and loss through both emotional and thinking processes, weighing the possibilities for accepting the difficult tension between them. The images of his pictures in "My Father's Photo Album" (page 135) reveal to the writer a new vision of her father as a young man long before her birth, and by shaking up our customary view of age and generations the poem becomes an illustration of the scientific notion of time as nonlinear.

Not incidentally, just because this or any other poem has a scientific, factual, or mental aspect neither means

Thoughts and ideas inform many, if not most, poems, though some are background or subtle sensibility while others are of central or topical importance.

126 ❧

it's a treatise nor precludes emotional impact. I could just as well have used "My Father's Photo Album" in Step 5 to talk about emotions (don't we all have intense feelings about the passage of time, mortality, and fathers?) just as I have shown "The Necessity" in both Steps. For me, the "facts" I learn from science or anywhere else are not necessarily the subjects I work with; instead, they give me exciting approaches to the images I see and the ways I feel about them, as in the parallel I draw in "Parhelion" (page 137) between "Barren galaxies / breed a trillion tons of stardust in a teaspoon" and "So anything I can imagine is possible, anything I dread."

What is more profoundly to the point than what information is used, or what is its source, is how the knowledge writers obtain from their readings, experience or interests gets shaped by their sensibilities and points of view and then inextricably kneaded into the bread of their poetry. Like emotions, sound, and other elements of prosody, ideas may make the physical poem rise in our minds, even if we can't readily glean or paraphrase them.

In fact when we read we may be so familiar with certain facts or understandings that we barely notice how a poem has built its foundation upon them. The poet makes use of those cultural common grounds, hoping to carry you along on them—or perhaps to startle you with new twists on old ideas, new connections, unexpected allusions, more potent images for grasping abstractions. It is a fountain of never-ending delight that a writer we like often has a recognizable "voice" throughout his various works, and that another writer, using the same

Like emotions, sound, and other elements of prosody, ideas may make the physical poem rise in our minds, even if we can't readily glean or paraphrase them.

language and form, can sound entirely different. These phenomena depend on how each mind constructs its own relationship to language, culture, and self.

They also depend on how the writer conveys that relationship. For instance, some poets blatantly advise us: "You must revise your life," said William Stafford. Of course the poet is probably mainly advising himself, but he's imparting the revelation he came to in the course of the poem's journey for our benefit as well. The thinking process the writer travels through is ours for the taking, whether it ends in wisdom or wonder, and whether it begins with a philosophy already believed at the outset, or essays through undecided territory toward a hope of finding answers.

"The Sleepwalker"(page 129) is one of the latter. Sleepwalking is often a metaphor for not knowing what we're doing. This poem is thinking about what it's like seeing someone we love suffer in his quest for self-discovery, and knowing, even when he doesn't, that he is learning all the while. Its triggering question (what I wrote the thing to figure out) was whether we should interfere—"help" him feel better, help him see what he's done—or hold back and let the person take the risks necessary to come to self-understanding in his own time. Although it looks like I started out with the answer to my doubts, in fact I didn't know it until I'd written through the whole poem. You can see that the final stanza is missing its fourth line to finish symmetrically with all the other quatrains; it migrated to become the opening line.

The Sleepwalker

Let him walk.

Though he knows nothing of it,
it's the one thing he does with ease.
So I keep myself
from calling out his name.

He doesn't see me, awake, beside him—
but I, like the true sleepwalker,
follow after him, out of doors,
over the rails, out into the danger

zones. Night after night, unafraid,
he goes looking; and I watch,
in order to be the one
who will remember.

He never knows why—
like the dancing princess who every night
wore out her newest shoes—
for him the mornings have no rest.

This is his other life,
the one he's never dreamed of,
in which he dares the darkness
and defies all heights.

I hold my breath
while he walks the precipice
with the acuity of the blessed.
They say

if you wake the sleepwalker,
he may fall; but sleeping,
he forgets he ever climbed at all.

By contrast, "No One There" (page 132) has a built-in idea. The complaint it explores is that in ostensibly only observing nature we readily change the act—if not the thing witnessed—into a reference to the self. Thus the observer's self-congratulatory inner monologue goes something like this: "Look at me, I am being struck by beauty. Yup, here I am, me, all alone in the vast world. Those trees I see in the woods are just like the ones in my imagination/memory/poem. Hm, why go out at all? I can depict in my personal way what is happening when I'm not even present to see it." Et cetera. Of course, the not-so-subtle irony in the poem is that it is doing exactly the same thing. It's an ages-old conundrum—observation/participation—not only in the work of artists but of scientists, and thinking about trying to escape it can make your head spin.

No One There

The sun is setting elsewhere in the woods and I hope
that no one is there to be struck
by slant rays or shade or by the sight
of trees rising in her own thoughts—I hope no one
is bearing witness to his vision or the damp whispers
of molten leaves under snow—this afternoon
whether a ruffed grouse or a hawk or an owl
lingers, lucky, in the eaves of a sunset,
whether footprints spray the snow with shadows
or the branches of dead oaks burst through the air—
I hope that no one is there
to dream about solitude and language
and the coming on of night.

In addition to ideas, philosophies and facts, poets love another kind of knowledge: the one that grows out of our imaginations. The human imagination lets us empathize with others experiencing things we never have, decide against a course of action because of its potential outcomes, invent or create new paintings, machines, sentences to communicate what we've been trying to tell someone. Using imagination, a poet can write in the voice or viewpoint of another person, a dragonfly, an alien, or a rock, or simply take herself to a new level of awareness.

In "Unfinished Poem" (page 138) I use imagination based on both my experience of what rock feels like (I like rocks) and my philosophy that living a full and true life means breaking loose from whatever actual or perceived (or subconscious) bonds prevent us from that powerful—and (here's that complexity again) vulnerable—freedom. So this poem is very much based on thought—an idea fleshed out in images, sensations, and feeling.

There is no end to the kinds and uses of ideas, knowledge, and thoughts in poems, but to make these accessible, undidactic, affecting, and even memorable, they ought to be dressed up in colorful clothes and not seen prancing down the street in the buff. In other words, let's hope they have sensory images, emotional draw, engaging language and form, and don't just lecture us with one finger wagging.

As you read a poem for the second or third time (not so much in the first run), pay attention to your thoughts as you figure out how the material can or cannot make

There is no
end to the
kinds and
uses of ideas,
knowledge,
and thoughts
in poems, but
to make these
accessible,
undidactic,
affecting,
and even
memorable,
they ought
to be dressed
up in colorful
clothes and
not seen
prancing down
the street in
the buff.

sense in your worldview. Is it confirming something you'd already contemplated, telling you something you hadn't quite thought of before, at least not in this way, or inspiring you to entirely revise your life? Is it OK to be led to think about uncomfortable issues and not given any conclusive closure? Is confusion of any use?

Try (and I mean this in both senses) your willingness to think with some other poems now. For example, look again at "Archaelogy" (Step 2, page 55). What idioms, information, references and assumptions do you recognize, and how are they used? You might try contemplating why the poem makes you think the thoughts you are thinking—wonder, instruction, juxtapositions, example, word choice? If you can, find out if yours are the same thoughts as a (real) person sitting next to you reading the same poem, and then see what *that* makes you think.

My Father's Photo Album:
Japan 1947

Here is the proof
of what's impossible to know:
Our parents when younger than we,
and ourselves when older than they.
You can barely touch it
without the black velvet pages,
heavy as handfuls of loam,
turning to weightless dust.

Here's the ship, with crowds of men, clouds
arranged about the masthead.
Friends with names like Newt and Chazz
pose with Japanese girls.
My father leans in close, holds a puppy
named after himself. Artful shots
of miniature bridge over stream,
curve of snow, fountain.

I read my father through his past,
which is my past. I use his eyes
then, in the future now:
That's the gift.
I enter through them, here, in this album
of focused views and clear wonder,
of certain youth, and an age
born old already from the human heart.

You can see how the children love him,
two bundled boys by a lamp-post,

a girl holding a smaller one, too shy to look.
They too speak with their eyes.
Here's a fish-market octopus, here a woman
kneeling by her baskets on the walk.
Rickshaw, thatched roof, baseball game.
Ruined building, bonsai, Russian troops.

Here are the modern streets of Tokyo,
a bride in traditional dress.
Here the farms at Akibane,
a "prize-winning" still life silhouette.
This is how they build with paper and wood.
This is how a young man—a boy—
his first time away from home—
sees his future back there.

When I see what he saw, I can almost believe
what the physicists say: that time moves
in both directions at once. Maybe it's true
that I'll grow old in the future, and wonder
about the past instead. Maybe it's true
that my father is no longer young with new
and watching eyes. Maybe I was always there
waiting to be looking back.

Parhelion

I saw the sky blow open from its center. I saw
the whole pasture bow down, like a ship before waves.
The sky began to expand, circling outward,
from memory toward prediction, in rounds of muted hues.
The damp air invited it, suppressed it, led it on.
Clouds—grayed pools of fingerpaint—spread,
collided, and splashed over mountainsides,
while planets swept along in spindrift until angels
fled their halfbright moons and rings.
If it went on like this, on a normal day,
the sky would vanish, leaving only the unbearable gaze,
the utterance of fossil and bone, the jagged edge
of broken sky in its complicated darkness,
and my own jagged edges, no longer eclipsed.
Always, I thought, there is a given, unempirical—
for instance the world, born from out of nothing,
the truly immaculate conception: an absolute
in direct relation to nothing. Barren galaxies
breed a trillion tons of stardust in a teaspoon.
So anything I can imagine is possible, anything I dread.
There are seashells in the hills, sundogs in heaven,
absolute good on earth—I believe it.
And what is beyond dream or horizon is on its way
back home. I call out to it. I expect it to answer.
The world is time, running in circles, catching its own tail.

Unfinished Poem

*After the Michelangelo sculptures, each called "The Captive,"
often referred to as "The Unfinished Sculptures"*

I'd imagine my way out of the stone.
First, I'd test every surface pressed against mine,
every edge and angle that I'm up against.
I'd test texture and position, concentrate
on solidity and weight. Inside, unseen
the stone is smooth and cool, the same
as my own skin. I can't define myself.
Below is a deep, frozen river,
where I've stood since time began.

Now—I want to get out.

I've begun to imagine how an arm would feel,
straight instead of bent, or a muscle, slack,
not pressing, not lifting, not pushing or resisting—
what an arm would do, free to rise by itself:
I've begun to believe in it.
I don't remember the sculptor's hands,
now gone to dust; my own body is still alive,
whole, the way I was imagined if not made,
the way I was found, and captured.

I am breaking for the utter sensation
of air and space and time, where nothing
is etched in stone, where the memory of stone
is a surface tension snapped by will:
a skin. Now my own arm, lifting

only against itself, the up against the down,
not against this dead weight. Yes,
I imagine myself, surrounded by all the blades
or air: unsheathed, unshielded, ready to be mortal.

Step 7

⚜ FICTION'S DEVICES ⚜

Poems Use Some of the Same Ploys as Prose

WHEN WE READ, we have expectations. Writers know that, and work to either thwart or reward them—or both. When you read a short story you expect to know who you're dealing with, and what the problem is, within maybe half a page, and the denouement (the clean-up after the climax) may be a mere sentence. If your novel is a long one, you can go a chapter or two before you want to feel sure of your footing, and the climax might still be followed by twenty pages or more.

Proportionately, we'll give a poem only a couple of lines before we need to at least get a feel for the landscape. Even though what is "happening" there and to whom may not be readable as a narrative storyline, and endings may vary from epiphany to cliff-hanger, most poems still have some kind of "arc."

The arc's main aspect is the accruing of "information" for you to process line by line. This progression will be influenced by syntactical continuity, which may have no blatantly stated connective tissue, or which may make use of cue words like "but," "so" and "then." Another aspect of the arc is a poem's reach: What does it aim for, how complex are its language, images, emotions and thoughts? How high does it carry you on the curve of all these elements, and how high or low are you left dangling when it is all over?

Let's climb on.

"Where's Papa going with that ax?" Fern says as we begin *Charlotte's Web*.

"Where's Papa going with that ax?" Fern says as we begin *Charlotte's Web*. Relationships already exist here, and not just among the people; "that ax" also has a history in this family. And right away, there's delicious tension.

Within the first line, "The Bat" (page 143) also establishes that there is already a relationship—"us"—for the reader to enter. Incidentally, there is always a "we" in any poem addressed to a "you," but there is also one even when the unspoken recipient is understood to be *you*, the ultimately addressed reader. In this case, by being privy to something about "us" you know there's a history, a back-story, though you know few if any details about it. What is not said—omission—and how you fill in those blanks—are integral parts of any story.

The Bat

Night came over us before the whole sky
had filled in at its fontanel.
Stars turned on near the horizon
like house lights, one by one,
and reckless moths crashed by.
In the valley, fireflies rose
over the old foundation.
The trees you'd tipped
cleared the distance of a darkness
deeper and farther away.

On the edge of the porch you built,
carefully slanted for run-off,
I sat, bare feet touching the dirt
and the wet grass that moved
beneath the night.
I wore the red cotton dress
with little white leaves printed on,
but the red, like the color of the sky,
had no color then. We called it "dark."

You, in cut-offs, stood on the hill
outside the circle of porch light.
We watched the bat, a darker spot
in the dull black air,
its quickness, sometimes,
more perfect than the eye's.
I could see you
but it was the darkness that he saw.
There was no sense in light.

You taught him a game,
throwing a stone straight into the sky
over your head.
He followed it up, arriving first
at the apex, then down, faster
than gravity, missing it on purpose
every time, flying
again and again between the stone
and its direction.

I waited for that thump that would bring
bat, stone, and your diversion
down to the earth at my feet.
You never tired, but for me
you were no less distant, no more solid,
than the darkness that was night's
definition. Surely bats know stones
don't fly. So he must have known
you were there—or someone
was there.

As is often the case in the opening paragraphs in fiction, the first stanza in "The Bat" lets you know of actions in the past, and describes a setting, in this case a rural or remote one, if stars are visible by the horizon. Clues to a time are also set—nightfall, summer (fireflies)—as well as a little of the history—the "you" has done some work clearing a better view—which later becomes a significant detail because it introduces the ironic theme of the poem. As the poem goes on into the second stanza, more information accrues about the person addressed, who is apparently aware of surroundings (literally broadening the view) and careful of doing things right (building the porch for proper drainage). Even the dress the speaker wears is part of their lives and past; if it weren't, it would be "a" dress, not "the." But if all this is so, what's wrong?

As we move into stanza three, something else is becoming clear—a distance between the two people suggested by other details of distance and closed vision in each stanza so far—and in stanza four the lingering action of the bat and the player echo each other and the images of the previous stanzas, both "characters" seeming to function on a kind of oxymoronic blind sight. Readers know that what a writer directs most of our time and attention to in detail, dialogue, or drama must be important to the story.

In the last stanza we know the speaker is unhappy with the game of connection/no connection, afraid for the bat while resentful of the attention it is getting. She finally—climax—comes right out and names the problem that's been stirring throughout the poem—that "you were no less distant, no more solid / than the darkness

The
speaker of
a poem—
any
poem—
has a voice,
and a
persona.

that was night's / definition." Who are you, the speaker seems to ask; how can we be this close and yet not know each other? Like the bat, she can only know that "someone / was there." Denouement.

The speaker of a poem—any poem—has a voice, and a persona. Even if the poet is not purposely channeling other psyches, but rather speaks of herself disingenuously as "I," that person is a fictional character her real friends, assuming she has any, might not totally recognize. As a reader, you decide if you trust that voice, the way she thinks, the things she has to say about her world. The writer manipulates you by trying to make you trust her persona. In "The Bat," readers probably take the side of the speaker, because that confiding first person point of view is the one you're automatically supposed to sympathize with. But what if we heard the story from the point of view of the one she's "talking to" in that woeful kind of too-late-now tone of hers? "Get over it," he might say. "I was just having a little fun; lighten up."

Less focused on a particular human relationship and more on the predicament of being human in general, "Roots" (page 147) works by a narrative-like progression of sentences, and its details, in particular the nouns, set this poem in an ancient timeframe. And yet that intimate "we" (you, the reader, are implicated in it), as well as certain phrases like "we pretend to be complete" and "where things are never said," along with the poem's mentioned effects of time on memory and imagination, tell us this may be a more contemporary and personal exploration of the self. No sense arguing which it's "supposed to be about"—it can, and should, very nicely be both.

Roots

I remember, we breathed water:
air came to us in disguise.
Then memory began attaching
its own vast reaches
to the not-yet human
imagination.
Some earthlike mass was where
we next went crawling,
dragging prehistory like seaweed
on useless gummy feet.
Now, we pretend to be complete.
The old rhythm nags at me,
wants to take me back
where things are never said
to solidify with time.
On the surface, even islands
may seem rooted,
though it be
to something unseen and oceanic.
All it is, is, they know
to stay aloof, aloft, afloat
in just one place,
treading water
in secret down below.

In both senses—ancient or contemporary—"Roots" moves from innocence to experience, in story-telling, syntactical form: from once upon a time—"I remember"—through "then," "next," and "now" to looking back with nostalgia or yearning and finally summing up with an image that illustrates a bitter, if funny, philosophy. The arc of the poem carries us from the remembered comfort of life back then through amphibious, difficult transformations to its conclusion—the struggle to stay afloat and make the only life or identity we have—"just one place"—look easy.

Another, this one with an O. Henry ending:

Barbed Wire

Before I had children I walked through the woods
beyond the pastures, where last century's fences
were once pushed against the bark of some young trees.
I saw how the trees had grown swollen around wires,
swallowed them and gone on ringing with their age.
I followed one wire to its disappearance
centered in a maple, as if it were incidental,
and I found where it emerged, clean, on the other side.
Sometimes the trees grew far and rich above the cut
hardened and healed before memory could stoop down
to listen, those branches in the sky oblivious
to this blemish, this gash, still visible at the level
of a child's eye. But I was not thinking of children then,
their soft flesh, impressionable, nor how fast
they grow around us, how miraculously tall
I have become.

STRANGE
TERRAIN

Step 7
FICTION'S
DEVICES

Where is
this going?
How
will it be
concluded?
Am I being
set up?
How will I
feel when
it's done?

While focusing on wires and trees, its visible and concrete subjects, "Barbed Wire" plays out an extended metaphor about how good children are at growing up despite the wounds they incur in the process. But the poem twists around on itself at the end—twice. With its slow and steady pace (pacing being another device of fiction), the only tension here is the subtle questioning readers are familiar with more as sensation than thought as they read: Where is this going? How will it be concluded? Am I being set up? How will I feel when it's done?—all of which keeps readers on their toes.

How does this tension happen? One major way is through syntax, specifically subclause: "Before I had children. . ." the poem begins. Instantly the implication is "that was then," thereby hanging the "what about now?" question in the air, so that throughout everything afterward readers are waiting for that shoe to drop. The poem continues in the past tense and it's not until line 13 that we come forward into the speaker's present mind. Language of time—"young," "age," "grew"—keeps us aware that we're still hearing an echo of the theme of children, not just taking a walk through an old woods boobytrapped with a long-gone farmer's wires.

Now in line 13 ("But I was not thinking. . ."—the writer's current reflection) we feel relief that we've finally come to the present, possibly the "answer" to the suspended question. Line 14 goes on directly addressing what the poem has suggested all along—the vulnerability of children—but just when we think the tension is all released, the next to last line slaps us with the uncomfortable fact that the speaker—and all parents whom children "grow around"—are themselves the wires, the wounders. The poem could have left us squirming there on "how fast / they grow around us" (this first person plural pointing its finger to include you, the reader, with the speaker) but instead it twists one more time with the line break after "how miraculously tall" and, with its subject switch from third person plural (they, the children) to first person singular, the final line that follows: "I have become."

The fact that, in reading, we identify with the implied or stated speaker, feeling her emotions, getting inside her head, is one reason reading is so affecting as well as morally instructive. The final line of "Barbed Wire" reminds us that parents are also grown children, that there is a chain of pain—and also growth: the poem does not judge, only leaves us grieving equally for our children as for ourselves.

It's not hard to see how the conventions of reading fiction are useful in reading poems that, however briefly and perhaps impressionistically, also tell stories. But poems use the devices of prose even when they are abstract and not directly about people and their relationships and mishaps. Ready to see how that works? Let's try it with "Now and Then" (page 152).

Now and Then

Slowly, it is dusk,
Morning,
Spring.
Now you notice, now
Believe in what you see.

You always miss that moment
Of things becoming right; the shift's
No sharper than memory's.
Or maybe nothing
Stirs at all,

But the thing you want to fix
Moves through space—fast,
But still, like starlight.
Imagine that you could trap it once
In a mirror balanced between

Now
And then. The mirror, for a moment,
Holds the two apart,
And holds
The parts together.

The poem identifies no one, but in fact speaks in the kind of second person that is not meant for a particular, closely related person so much as to address both the self and the other (reader) as one. This sets up a simultaneous and contradictory intimacy and distance which precisely mimics the sense of the poem itself. As you read the poem, see if you can feel your readerly expectations, your inner questions as you look around: Where am I? What's going on? Is anybody there?

Time is shifting out of my grasp here, you might say. *Just when I've established that it's dusk, it's morning. Oh, now it's spring. How did that happen?*

Exactly. Right away, the poem is trying to disorient us, slip between our fingers; it repeats what happens to us, how we will notice it is spring, though we missed its becoming so. In its various ways, "Now and Then" says that "now" almost is "then," that we only see the present when it has passed, and wish it could be otherwise.

How else does the poem explore this idea? What is the conundrum of the mirror?

I never intended "Now and Then" to be about the act of reading, but it might almost be. Even in this rarified realm, the poem progresses sentence by sentence and line by line, and that's how you seem to take it in. Yet just as with the awareness of time, you don't know you've "got it" until after the fact. While you are reading, whether novel or poem, you constantly move pieces of information to make room for the next item, at the same time reassessing what you already have in the light of this newest addition. Your mind is not only moving forward in this

While you are reading, whether novel or poem, you constantly move pieces of information to make room for the next item, at the same time re-assessing what you already have in the light of this newest addition.

process, but circling back and around the entire territory of what you've read, what you've experienced that it connects with, and what you are guessing is yet to come. So much for the linear theory of time.

Step 7
FICTION'S
DEVICES

Wintering

When it comes breaking the sky
in two, I hear it first
and face the wind to wait.
I squint past where eyesight fails,
rooted to the ground in winter
seedlings of rye,
tasting the crisp and sunshot
apple-cold air—and there—
the line of geese
appears, waving like heat
leaving for the south.
Last night six deer met in the yard,
two of them too small for wintering.
Maybe strewn fruit and cabbage stems
give them some animal equivalent
of hope. They must know,
the way that these things know,
that this is the season to die.
But then death
always travels alongside us,
close as peripheral vision.
There are ways of living
through these days of dark and cold.
Go underground, build shelter, trust
in windfall. Look out for the horizon
spinning south like geese,
for that glassy yellow light,

for frost embalming the grass.
Wait, slowly, and stay in this world
with me,
searching the distance for a way
to live in place
of giving in.

Step 8

🌱 UNKNOWING 🌱

Poems Can
Mystify You

LINEAR TIME—RIGHT: IS this physics? Logic: Statistical analysis? Emotional sensitivity: Psychotherapy? *I thought this was a book on how to appreciate poetry: English.* What's going on here?

Let's back up a minute.

Unlike prose, poetry has little time or room in its compressed language and form for asides, explanations, and lengthy musings; everything has to cohere intensively in the service of the poem's intentions. Unlike in political or commercial talk, with which we are inundated, poetry's is a language of concision and precision that imparts not less than it literally means but more than it verbally says. Unlike in much of our social lives, where

Unlike in political or commercial talk, with which we are inundated, poetry's is a language of concision and precision that imparts not less than it literally means but more than it verbally says.

🌱 157

So damn right
you're confused.
And what are
you going to do
about it?

Nothing.

a whole lot of talk goes on without a whole lot being said, in a single poem you can take in so much with so brief a time for processing that you may end up feeling overwhelmed—because, unlike in math, poetry adds up to a total greater than the sum of its parts. It is the nearly infinite complexity of its shape, language, sounds, images, emotions, thoughts, and literary devices and it still is more than that.

So damn right you're confused. And what are you going to do about it?

Nothing.

In this section I am not going to tell you how not to feel confused, unsettled or unsure after reading a poem. I am going to validate your confusion and tell you that it is all right if you feel that way. The fact is, it's a non-problem.

Remember that poems are often produced from that same "unknowing" state of mind. Poet Franz Wright describes his as a "deliberate unconsciousness of subject material." That's how amazing things can get said, surprising even the writer. Wright says he allows a level of "conscious awareness" to enter only "very late in the process."

If writers are channeling their poems through a psychic, mystical, or other non-linear, non-thought-based process, only in the final exertions using the sweat of conscious revision to make just as much tangible sense as seems necessary to shape a new, true whole—well then, some of that lack of "knowing" is probably going to linger in the finished product.

I prefer to think of it as an alternative kind of knowing. It's not one that gets a lot of credit in our culture.

Tyrannical logic reigns in our daily lives. Also sneaking in frequent appearances is a particular lack of logic we might call stupidity. Poetry's brand of reason is neither of these. Its carriage of meaning rolls along on wheels of intuition, is-ism, truth and mystery, and what it conveys, even if we can't name it, is something we cannot sensibly live without.

It's complicated. Most significant things are. The details of our lives—the trillium flowering under a fern, the way your father held his glass when he drank, the mud on your boots—the experience—the suffering, the thrill—of being alive, here, now, like every other living thing and like no one and nothing else: Poetry draws us out of our automatic-pilot, running-around-unsmell-ingly-through-the-roses and into the physical, messy, exquisite reality of who we are—not what we know or do or what we're supposed to do next, but what it feels like to be.

Every detail that a poem describes or illustrates in sentences or in sound is a package, an onionate gift. You feel and you remember and you associate and you feel again. Then you have a thought and then you have another you can't really put your finger on. You have a flash of something you can't quite remember but you're reminded of it anyway. You yearn, you regret, you recognize, you anticipate, you miss, you wish. You fill up, you overflow, you empty. You're lost, you're four again, you're ecstatic, you're scared. It just goes on and on, like Life.

Is that not a knowing? Did you expect it to be simpler? We all have our limits. We will turn off if it's all too

. . . what it conveys, even if we can't name it, is something we cannot sensibly live without.

Every detail that a poem describes or illustrates in sentences or in sound is a package, an onionate gift.

🌼 159

much with us. The full appreciation of poetry will take time and practice, like the building up of a formerly flaccid muscle or the perfection of an étude or a figure-skating routine. How much time—and accompanying ache—will depend on your tolerance level of things simultaneously unexplainable and affecting, how much "unknowing" you want to know.

The sensation of unknowing you feel at the end of a poem is not something you get and then get over. You just improve your ability to accept it. Then—*ooh*—you start really liking it. Then, you hope for it. Eventually, you're disappointed if the poem doesn't help you achieve it.

What's required is, yes, similar to what the therapists call "sitting with your feelings." Let's call it "sitting with your poem." If you practice your unknowing tolerance level, you will not only get comfortable with and appreciative of poetry, thereby broadening and enriching your life and impressing people at parties; you may even get along better with your significant other and your boss. You'll be able, in general, to tolerate more uncertainty, fewer answers, more unfixables, less linear logic, more stimulation of what-ifs, and have less fear of strangeness. Strangeness is a jolt of Oh!—a punch-line, a vacation, a wake-up call. We get to feel refreshed and freed from habits. Isn't that why we sometimes go looking for strange terrain?

In the Kabbalah, the ancient mystical Jews believed that the letters of the alphabet depicted God's visage, which, paradoxically, no mortal can behold. Reading, they taught, is a holy act because in it you see the presence of God.

Some of the most life-affirming, necessary things in the world cannot be thoroughly explained, or can only be "understood" through intuitive acceptance of their mystery. Poetry, as ancient as human love, art, or a sense of the spiritual, is one of them. So be curious. Aim for what the scientist Lewis Thomas wonderfully called "enlightened bewilderment." Learn as many concrete clues as you can, sidle up to the challenge by means of whatever route you stumble across, approaching obliquely with brave baby steps. Then stare into the eye of wonder, surrender, and let it take you from there.

No Less

It was twilight all day.

Sometimes the smallest things weigh us down,
small stones that we can't help
admiring and palming.

Look at the tiny way
this lighter vein got inside.
Look at the heavy gray dome of its sky.

This is no immutable world.
We know less than its atoms, rushing through.

Light, light. Light as air, to them,
for all we know. Trust me on this one,
there is happiness at stake.

Boulder, grain. Planet, dust:
What fills the stones fills us.

I remember, or I have a feeling,
I could be living somewhere with you,
burdened in a way we aren't now.

Often the greatest things,
those you'd think would be the heaviest,
are the ones that let us rise.

Fireflies

It had to do with light.
It had to do with open doors,
with darkness and motion, with light.

A dark road, unpaved,
and just us walking to a meadow
opening from trees, an expanse

that in memory fills the world,
crowds trees and homes
so far into the edges
that they become merely frame.

The field was dark but not alone;
it was full, and moving.
It moved upward, it pulled me upward,
drew the grasses upward,

into the bottomless skies.
Fireflies—shadowless—
lifting the air on blinking wings

rose, each flash streaking
the whole globe upward
in light brush strokes. We saw

the earth rising like dust motes, unearthly,
the sky rising like starlight,
skyward. We collided there

with the light and silence
exploding the air,
uprooting trees and grasses and heaving earth.

In that moment I regretted our unlived lives,
sad moons eclipsed,
and I saw through them,
darkness lit from the inside.

Elemental

It is never a question of wanting to fall.
It is the precipice which calls, the air
that yearns for the body to caress.
As heaven meets the upward
gaze of earth, and as all land
is water bound, so I am defined by you.
The drowning man pulls up the sea
like bedclothes, and finally is buoyant.
Profiles of the beach—all area
momentarily outlined, then merely memorized:
Once something else, now beautiful. Here
new agates grow unknown, like their aired
ancestors, the arrowheads on drier sand.
Even these stones have always known
where they are going.
They're in no hurry, we don't name them
—or love them—for their descent.
It's elemental.
I'm not talking about the crash.
I mean passion, the wave following
its heart, airborne: No turning back,
no questions asked.

How To Live

In northern plains grass grows only
for the reindeer. The grass gives
them strength enough to live
till invisible flies come
and run them to their deaths.

At war, soldiers cease
to reason, but differently
from the dancers and the mountain
climbers whose bodies
know what freedom is.

Love is as semaphoric.

All things are of two
natures. For identification,
one remains with the body, held
for safekeeping. The second
is for the living, for the knowing

how to live
without knowing how.

On Your Own

IN THIS SECTION you will find poems mentioned in the "Introduction to a Poet"(page 11) as well as one "bonus" poem you haven't heard a thing about—other than all the elements of prosody that went into making it which you now understand. These and all the other poems waiting for you around the world are yours for you to read with your new skills and renewed sense of wonder, at your own pace, whenever you want to go there.

Stone Walls

He wants to build stone walls with his father.
He wants to reconstruct the legacy of old stones,
clear the land and weight it down
around its edges. He wants to take in hand
the cool rough bark of rock, soothe it
in uplifted palms.
He wants to lift the heaviest ones,
to learn the feel of balance and the heft of space.
He wants to place the stones one by one
in a structure of rows where one won't count,
so that the strength of number holds,
and leans in on itself. He wants to pass the stones
in silence, hand to hand, in agreement
with their perfect fit.
He wants to work the stones just so,
to make a thousand framed keyholes of air.
He wants to build the hard, silent, heavy
walls of stone around a common land,
letting each stone linger in an open hand,
unique and familiar as home.

Unlocking

But it is not always quiet here.
Things go on while we sleep the sleep of soldiers.

Ancient branches crack and splinter into dust.
Large wings snap open in spring
like carpets splayed out over the railing.

Granite splits apart at the seams
and great animals cleave roads through woods.

Daily, in the density, there is life
on the edge of the knife that cuts the world
into hemispheres of sense and death.

Trees are born and die, bones turn to humus,
glaciers to meadowland. It is time

to turn yourself loose, like new leaves,
like big lakes on which swim enormous birds
at a distance deeper in breadth than the water's depth.

Their shadows pull you to the shore.
Their size fills your lungs with sky. It is time

to heave aside the boulders and the dams,
to come back out like a bear after the thaw, to be
ready for the forest, for the forage, for the full

and waning moons. You will get soaked in wet grass,
feel the insects pierce your skin. You will learn

to balance between gravity and light. There will be
hot and sticky nights, sharp songs at dawn,
long and bright ineffable days.

This is your chance to crash your way
through underbrush unlocking like so many doors.

What Birds Hear

Way above the forests and plains,
forests and plains sculpt space.
That's what birds hear. Air.

So air must be a map,
a geology of silence: It lacks
only the sound of words.

Arctic ice floes are flown by loons in Maine,
and other oceans are shown to teals in waves
of air above the Atlantic.

Now the distant rise and fall of land
announces itself here
in the rhythms of herons in flight.

To birds, the turns and tones of air
are clear geographies
read—like braille—by their wings.

They hear what we can't hear or see—
what we never imagine. Air.
And they sing.

Bells without a Church

The angels are out on Wednesday Hill.
Here, the thousands of Queen Anne's lace
singing with a sound like rain, like yes.
They're rising tall above the field,
nodding—large, then small, until
a mist in the distance.
This is their meadow, their church,
as you are mine, the element
I become, unlaced. Your hands
the hands of the sky.
Those ladies and I—
blithely in the air without wings,
ringing without bells, sailing on high
without seas. . . . For a spell,
the line between this feat and me
flies bright, invisible as pollen:
A life all its own.

Spring,

you come made of whole cloth, like a child,

familiar unfathomable. I can't take my eyes
off you. Spring, spinning spun
of patience urgency, electric mild,

you are a new life
better than mine, less afraid, less induced
by fear, more sloppily insistent, more happily unabashed.

How blessed you are,
you do not call yourself by human name
or count your days in numbers.

I call you
a way of life, intricate plain, and fervent.
You reach down

around and through me, and needle the snow,
and underneath its quilt
come forth the green tongues telling

their one secret, memorized always new.
I overhear it; I believe it.
I wing on the breeze like blankets

left to fly off the line. Spring,
you befall me like child's play
and I fall for it every time, every

last moment of you. Your commandment
never balks, never passes, it can't wait.
It arrives with forewarning out of the blue,

woven out of winter hurtling toward heat,
glacial eruptive. Spring, my favorite one,
you are a time,

you are noun verb, you are a weight
that gravity can't take. You evaporate
age from my pores, the way April

dries my hair in the plush loft of its air,
as if you had offered your arms and taken up
in your many hands the weak, the wet.

Oh, I am grateful
for many things, but none more than this:
this unownable gift of life

and I will save it just as it saves me,
for when this brief season goes
I will catch its last thread unraveling,

I will sew it onto the wind,
I will pass it back through my heart.

The White and Frozen Place

So much snow falling becomes
One snowfall, one winter, lengthening

The shadows of things caught
In a day's last light.

Even the dead trees
By some trick of light
Seem to grow once more.

So much room

Between the four winds crossing one another
Like familiar enemies.

So much frost and forgetting
Where the heart is.

Under a halo of woodsmoke

Someone adds dry twigs to a fire
Designed to melt the dense season, inseparable
From the lost heart.

Someone, maybe,
Who knows about breaking ice floes, the silence
Of new growing things,

And the sudden recognition
Of once forgotten footprints.

It is a long walk back
Over such deep snow, such a white and frozen place.

Of the Heart

In the heart, we expect to meet
what is waited for around corners.
And what we leave behind
is still ahead, like the sailor's home
as he sails around the world.

The heart is a mirror, you said.
In it we know what can't be known
with any other part of the body.

I see the evergreens following you
up beyond the timberline.
Together you climb
on to where the horizon
blends with all the rest.

Down below, entire landscapes move
with the indifference of passersby.
Marsh becomes meadow, mountains bloom
into breeze. Those trees
run about the hills like antelope!

The sky is shining like silvered glass.
I see you in it, and know.

How to Keep Poetry in Your Life

IN ADDITION TO a rich spectrum of books about poetry, there are more poems out there than anyone could hope to consume. Go back to the classics like Shakespeare, Blake and Yeats, and the old bookstore standbys like Emily Dickinson and Robert Frost. Don't forget poets in translation. Also show up to listen at open mikes at the artsy coffee shops, or pick up contemporary poetry collections from the many dedicated small presses that publish it, as well as the bountiful little magazines, journals, and anthologies at your local booksellers or libraries. You will see how alive and well the world of poetry is these days.

You will also find an abundance of poetry online. Here are two sites for poems galore. Poetry Daily, at www.poems.com, will keep you up to date on what's being published right now in the small presses. Poetry Out Loud, at www.poetryoutloud.org/poems, has a listing of hundreds of poems from several centuries, put out by the National Endowment for the Arts and the National Poetry Foundation.

Following is a fairly random list of living English-speaking authors writing in a variety of styles, some easier or more challenging than others, whose works have enriched my life and might do the same for yours. And just in case you still aren't sure if it's OK not to be sure of the terrain when you're reading a poem, I offer one last fun fact: Former United States Poet Laureate Robert Hass put together a book of poems culled from his wide-ranged readings in contemporary poetry, called *Poet's Choice,* which I also recommend to you. For each selection, this most poetically knowledgeable guide writes a helpful, thoughtful morsel of an introduction; in one of these he tells us, "I don't completely get this poem."

In no particular order:

Mary Ruefle	Thylias Moss
Ben Lerner	Jane Miller
Kazim Ali	Rita Dove
Renee Ashley	Brenda Hillman
H. L. Hix	Robert Wrigley
Jim Schley	Kimiko Hahn
Mark Doty	Stuart Dischell
Jane Hirshfield	Kevin Young
Carl Phillips	James Galvin
Li-Young Lee	Jane Mead
Sandra Alcosser	Patricia Smith
Tony Hoagland	Jean T. Day
Rebecca Seiferle	Elisabeth Robinson

Optional Ramblings

Suggestions for Discussions & Syllabi

Questions & Activities for Individual Readers, Teachers, Discussion Leaders & Self-Directed Reading Groups

WHILE AN APPRECIATION of poetry is a worthy goal unto itself, the skills it develops extend into other realms of reading, writing, analysis and awareness—an education valuable to all.

Toward these ends, one way to tackle this book and its ideas is to start your meeting (note to individual readers: Please adapt group suggestions for your own use) with a volunteer reading aloud, and without comment, the first poem featured in the chapter or Step under discussion for the day. Then, together, read the chapter up to that poem, slowly and carefully following the guidance through it. Stop whenever someone has a thought, question, or comment. State your responses for all to hear, allowing for differing views of the poem and its elements, and not getting too bogged down in personal stories on the subject of a poem. Some readers will become explicators or defenders of a particular poem, or aspect of it, while others will be challengers or questioners.

STRANGE
TERRAIN

*Optional
Ramblings*

SUGGESTIONS
FOR
DISCUSSIONS
& SYLLABI

Allow for argument—but be nice! And remember that it's fine not to like every poem you read.

If interest in a discussion lags, move on. Be thoughtful of others, and time constraints, and never let the masses get bored by beating a dead horse. Better to leave them (and yourself) with questions spinning through wide-awake heads than falling asleep over poetry. In classrooms, if using oral presentations, vary assignments so each student presents one of his own choice.

* * *

The following questions and activities can be modified as desired as essay assignments or as group-discussion spurs. I recommend that teachers explore them as well, by which I mean, teachers, that you do the assignments along with the students, and share your process so they don't start believing poetry has an authoritative guidebook secret only to you.

1 *Experiences with Poetry*

   a. What are your negative experiences with poems? Think of classroom settings as well as any others where you might have had a bad experience with a poem.

   b. What could have been done differently to make it a better experience?

2 *Who are Poets? Stereotypes*

   a. Are all poets alcoholics, depressed, nerdy, self-absorbed, intellectual, deep, emo, or artistic? Do you admire any of these traits or disdain them? What other stereotypes about poets do we tend to have?

   b. Locate a poet in your community and find out if he or she fits any of the stereotypes. To do this, use research, an interview, gossip, and your own intuition, as well as

an investigation into some of his or her poems. What can
you tell about a poet by reading his or her poems? Invite
your local poet in to read to the class and talk.

3 *A Process and a Passion for Each of Us*

*Optional
Ramblings*

SUGGESTIONS
FOR
DISCUSSIONS
& SYLLABI

a. Read the last few paragraphs at the end of the "Intro-
duction to a Poet and the Writing Process" (page 11),
describing how the author creates a poem. Compare her
process to one of your own when you are creating some-
thing. Where she says, "Words . . . are fabulous company"
substitute something you love in place of "words." (You
can change "are" to "is" if necessary to complete the
sentence.) Examples: "Baseball bats," "egg beaters," "oil
paints," "dancing," etc. Write 1–3 paragraphs about how
that feels to you. Share these with the class or group.

b. How does it feel to experience the fabulous company of
something that other people around you don't? Have
you ever heard them talk about their particular passions?
Which seems more important to you: to have the same
passion as people you like, or to know that you each have
one of your own?

4 *Don't Expect to Get It*

In "Poetry Is an Art" (page 23), the author says, "When I read
a poem, I don't expect to get it." Discuss your response to
this. How does it affect how you'll read a poem next time?
What does she want to get from a poem?

* * *

The following assignment (#5) can be utilized for each of
Strange Terrain's eight Steps, and can be done over and over
again with different poems every time, always with new results

🌿 183

Optional
Ramblings

SUGGESTIONS
FOR
DISCUSSIONS
& SYLLABI

and insights. In a reading group or a classroom, assign a new person to be responsible for leading each Step. A new poem can be responded to by each person, or, alternatively, the same single poem can be read by eight different people, one for each of the Steps.

5 *A Walk through a Poem*

a. Find a poem that you feel particularly illustrates the Step under discussion, or choose any poem at random to discover whether it does. Hint: If you admire or are intrigued by anything in the poem, or connect to what it's about, your enthusiasm will make the next part easier for both you and your listeners. On the other hand, it's always fun to discover in a poem things you never saw there until you had to look.

b. Lead your audience (in writing or orally) through the poem line by line with your personal view of how the poem accomplishes your assigned Step's aspect and how overall it has an effect on you. You don't have to say something about every line, but do let your discussion unfold in the natural way it would be read.

c. Another variation of this assignment is to ask three different people to be responsible for each Step. Each of the three works independently on the same poem, and then together, without prior consultation, they present the poem in front of the group as a team of coaches or travel guides through the poem. Most likely, their readings will overlap in some ways and differ in others. If any of the three find the poem lacking in that Step's aspect, let that view be defended and argued amongst the three, for the whole group to witness. Afterward, open up the discussion for all and see what the consensus is on the poem's success.

6 _Author/Reader Challenge_

Assign or choose a poem. Have one person or team be the readers and responders, and a second person or team pretend to be the writer of the poem. Person 1 will read the poem aloud and respond to it. Then the "writer" will tell if the reader is seeing all the elements the writer wanted to include, and if the reader's interpretation is grounded in what's actually present in the poem.

The "writer" must try to be clear on the difference between what's really on the page and what the intention of the author might have been. The reader is free to argue for anything he feels is happening in this poem, as long as he can "prove," by means of any or all of the Steps, that it's there. If the reader says, "This poem made me feel sad," the "writer" can say, "I was sad when I wrote it" or "I wanted you to feel sad," or even "If you're feeling sad, that's because your girlfriend just dumped you, because there's nothing sad about this poem." Reader and "writer" must support what they say by showing where in the poem their view is written.

Remember that there is no real right answer or key to a poem, but that the challenge here is in the hazy line between what we bring to our readings and what we "see" in the poem itself. This activity sharpens skills in our awareness of both.

This assignment can be raucously fun if the reader tries to be as outlandish as possible in his interpretations, so that the "writer" has to "convince" him of an entirely different intent. After the debate, let the listeners vote for who has been most convincing.

A final variation on this exercise is to mimic an old contestant game: Have three different possible "authors" of the poem. Each one gives his or her defense or explanation in response to readers' interpretations or comments. At the end, based on

STRANGE
TERRAIN

_Optional
Ramblings_

SUGGESTIONS
FOR
DISCUSSIONS
& SYLLABI

who was most convincing, the listeners will vote for who they think the "real" author was.

STRANGE
TERRAIN

*Optional
Ramblings*

SUGGESTIONS
FOR
DISCUSSIONS
& SYLLABI

7 *Surprises and Lessons*

What aspects of reading and understanding poetry surprised you in this book (or in a Step of the book)? Which did you realize you already knew? What did you learn about yourself as a reader? As a person?

8 *Teaching Each Other*

Use your class or reading group to teach each other: Ask any questions about understanding poetry that you still feel are unanswered. Give others a chance to share their thoughts on these questions. How do you think *Strange Terrain*'s author would answer your questions?

9 *Degrees of Mystery*

After reading Step 8, look back at what you wrote about for Assignment #3. Think about a creative endeavor that you know a lot about and have worked to be good at. Whether you are watching someone else do it or doing it yourself, how do you feel about whether there is still a degree of mystery or the unexplainable? For instance, if you are talented at drawing, or never miss hitting a pitch, and someone asks you how you do that, can you answer that question? What would you say? What other things have you experienced that cannot be fully explained or taught? How do you feel about them? What does this say about those things? About you?

* * *

Sessions of Various Durations

Note: It is important *not* to include readings of participants' own poetry, and *not* to host any time for writing with this program. *Strange Terrain* is not a writing manual, and programs based on the book are not intended to be writing workshops; including poetry writing will discourage the attendance of the very people who can most benefit by participating. Remember that this is a guide to the reading and appreciation of published poetry, and it is meant especially for those who are not as at ease with poetry as they would like to be.

Single Evening or 2-Hour Session

Read the book first and come prepared to discuss 3–4 poems, either from the book or your own selections, going through the Steps one by one in order, and combining some of the Steps as necessary.

5-Session Program, 1–2 Hours Each Day

For the first day, prepare to discuss the introductory chapters, and people's issues with poetry. Read at least one or two poems but don't discuss them. Each day thereafter, discuss two Steps, in order, and read several poems focusing on those Steps. Allow time for discussion and differing readings.

9-Week Program

Introductory chapters for Week 1, with discussion suggestions 1–4 above. Each subsequent week, delve into one Step. For each Step, read or review the chapter together after it's been read at home, discuss the poems and ideas, and try activities 5, 6 and 7. Assignments 8 and 9 come in the final week. Always provide resources for students to choose and explore poems on their own.

STRANGE
TERRAIN

*Optional
Ramblings*

SUGGESTIONS
FOR
DISCUSSIONS
& SYLLABI

Other ways to expand on the book for full-length sessions like this, particularly in high school and college courses:

— Have participants find or choose poems from a collection of published poems (contemporary or past), and/or from journals or anthologies—your decision. Use these with Steps of the process;

— If the HS or college course includes writing, after studying and reading examples of each Step you can let students write a poem of any kind illustrating that Step's points. In workshops, critique poems with those points in mind, building week by week to see if any one poem can embody every aspect.

Full Semester Program

Use the guideline above for the 9-week program, doubling the time for each Step. If your class meets only twice a week, the 9-week program will easily expand into 18 weeks. Adjusting for time involves simply adding to or decreasing the use of assignments and the number of poems presented or discussed. Also include listening to recordings of poets and inviting local or other poets in for readings and discussions.

If your full-semester course is a survey of poetry including how to understand it *and* how to write it, it's important to *complete the entire 9-week program above first*, without any writing yet, and then repeat the Steps, this time with writing by the students.

* * *

If Classes Do Include Writing
(And a Final Note on the Desired Outcomes of This Book)

As I've said above, I urge you to complete the course for *reading* poetry first. Even in creative writing classes, it's important to convey standards, and this book offers a guide to writers as well as readers. Familiarizing—inundating!—students with poetry's forms, sounds, language use, imagery, emotional and intellectual and literary measures, as well as its mystery, sends the crucial message that poetry, like ballet, is an art and a craft with particular, learnable skills for both practitioners and appreciators, and not simply an exercise in self-expression with no standards.

If everyone already knew that to be the case, this book would not have been necessary. The fact is that rather than diminishing or discouraging an interest in poetry, this knowledge comes as a relief to most people because it lets them know why they may not have understood poetry before, that their frustration was not a sign of any personal shortcoming, and that the problem can be remedied with some specific lessons.

Even those students who identify themselves as poets, once they've practiced the Steps of this book in their readings of poems, will feel a greater connection to their ancestral and global literary family, avoiding solipsism, and be inspired to take their writing farther than a single draft.

And once nonpoets have learned the actual techniques and elements of poetry found here, they will have increased their literacy, boosted their confidence, peaked their greater appreciation, grown into new readers and broader thinkers, sporting a deeper awe for this universal, age-old art. They will have launched themselves on an enduring journey through life's strange terrain.

STRANGE
TERRAIN

*Optional
Ramblings*

SUGGESTIONS
FOR
DISCUSSIONS
& SYLLABI

Acknowledgments

The poems by Alice Fogel used in this book previously appeared in two of her poetry books: *Elemental* (1993, Zoland Books), and *I Love This Dark World* (1996, Zoland Books).

Notes

About the Author

ALICE B. FOGEL is the author of three books of poetry, most recently *Be That Empty*, which stood four weeks on the National Poetry Foundation bestseller list in 2008. Her poems have appeared in many journals and anthologies, including the *Best American Poetry* series and former Poet Laureate Robert Hass's *Poet's Choice*. Recipient of an Individual Artist's Fellowship from the National Endowment for the Arts, among other awards, she teaches writing, literature, and other arts for all ages. In a different vein, Alice creates clothing, primarily out of "reprised" materials (www.lyriccouture.com), and leads workshops on refashioning. She has taught the *Strange Terrain* content to readers, learners, and teachers in a variety of venues, and is available for consultations or programs. For more information, or for further guidance reading, discussing, or teaching *Strange Terrain*, please visit www.alicebfogel.com.

READERS WHO ENJOYED *STRANGE TERRAIN*
MAY ALSO ENJOY *THE POEM AS A MARBLE, OR
HOW TO READ A POEM*, A TONGUE-IN-CHEEK
ESSAY BY SIDNEY HALL JR., AVAILABLE AS AN
EBOOK ON THE HOBBLEBUSH BOOKS WEB SITE.

WWW.HOBBLEBUSH.COM